On This

Photo courtesy of Stephen Ferry

On This Side of the River

SELECTED POEMS

David Ferry

WAYWISER

First published in 2012 by

THE WAYWISER PRESS

Bench House, 82 London Road, Chipping Norton, Oxon OX7 5FN, UK
P.O. Box 6205, Baltimore, MD 21206, USA
http://waywiser-press.com

Editor-in-Chief
Philip Hoy

Senior American Editor
Joseph Harrison

Associate Editors
Eric McHenry   Clive Watkins   Greg Williamson

ISBN 978-1-904130-52-9

Printed and bound by
T.J. International Ltd., Padstow, Cornwall, PL28 8RW

To my family

Stephen, Elizabeth, David, Sebastian, and Isaiah

and in memory of Anne Ferry

You lie in our bed as if an orchard were over us.
You are what's fallen from those fatal boughs.
Where will we go when they send us away from here?

Acknowledgements

REPRINTED BY KIND PERMISSION OF MARIE-HÉLÈNE GOLD

Arthur R. Gold's poems, "Chest Cancer," "Trolley Poem," and "On the Beach at Asbury," originally published in Gold's *Poems Written During a Period of Sickness* (Firefly Press, Somerville, MA, 1989).

REPRINTED BY KIND PERMISSION OF FARRAR, STRAUS AND GIROUX, LLC

"Spring" and "Orpheus and Eurydice" from *The Georgics of Virgil: Bilingual Edition* translated by David Ferry. Copyright © 2005 by David Ferry.

"Your Personal God" from *The Epistles of Horace: Bilingual Edition* by David Ferry. Copyright © 2001 by David Ferry.

"To Varus" from *The Odes of Horace: Bilingual Edition* translated by David Ferry. Copyright © 1997 by David Ferry.

"The Death of Enkidu" from *Gilgamesh: A New Rendering in English Verse by David Ferry.* Copyright © 1992 by David Ferry.

REPRINTED BY KIND PERMISSION OF CHICAGO UNIVERSITY PRESS

All other poems and translations in this selection, taken from David Ferry's *Bewilderment: New Poems and Translations*, *Of No Country I Know: New and Selected Poems and Translations*, *Dwelling Places: Poems and Translations*, *Strangers: A Book of Poems*, and *On the Way to the Island.* Copyright © 2012, 1999, 1993, 1983, 1960 by David Ferry.

ALSO BY DAVID FERRY

POETRY AND TRANSLATIONS

Bewilderment: New Poems and Translations 2012

The Georgics of Virgil 2005

The Epistles of Horace 2001

Of No Country I Know: New and Selected Poems and Translations 1999

The Eclogues of Virgil 1999

The Odes of Horace: A Translation 1997

Dwelling Places: Poems and Translations 1993

Gilgamesh: A New Rendering in English Verse 1992

Strangers: A Book of Poems 1983

On the Way to the Island 1960

PROSE

The Limits of Mortality: An Essay on Wordsworth's Major Poems 1959

Contents

The square-bracketed date shown after each title indicates the year of publication of the volume in which the poem (or a later revision) was first collected. A curly-bracketed name indicates the author or text or language of a poem in translation.

I

Contents

II

Contents

III

IV

V

Contents

VI

VII

VIII

Contents

IX

X

Contents

Narcissus

There's the one about the man who went into
A telephone booth on the street and called himself up,
And nobody answered, because he wasn't home,
So how could he possibly have answered the phone?
The night went on and on and on and on.
The telephone rang and rang and nobody answered.

And there's the one about the man who went
Into the telephone booth and called himself up,
And right away he answered, and so they had
A good long heart-to-heart far into the night.
The sides of the phone booth glittered and shone in the light
Of the streetlight light as the night went echoing on.

Out in the wild hills of suburban New Jersey,
Up there above South Orange and Maplewood,
The surface of a lonely pond iced over,
Under the avid breath of the winter wind,
And the snow drifted across it and settled down,
So at last you couldn't tell that there was a pond.

To Cornelius Nepos

– Catullus I

Who is it I should give my little book to,
Smoothed by pumice and polished to make it so pretty?

Cornelius, I'll give my book to you:
Because you used to think my nothings somethings,

At the time when you were the first in Italy
To dare to write our whole long history,

By Jupiter, three volumes under his sign,
Heroically achieved; so take this little

Book of mine for what it's worth, whatever;
And oh, patroness Virgin, grant that it

Shall live to survive beyond the century.

Found Single-Line Poems

TURNING EIGHTY-EIGHT, A BIRTHDAY POEM:

It is a breath-taking, near-death, experience.

FOUND POEM:

You ain't seen Nothing yet.

FOUND POEM:

We're all in this apart.

A SUB-TITLE:

Playing with My Self

One Two Three Four Five

anger

Anger is what I don't know what to do with.
I know it was anger was the trouble that other time.
I don't know where the anger came from, that time,
Or where it was I was going on anger's back
On a mission to somewhere to get me through the danger.

whatever

Whatever it is I think I probably know.
However whatever it is I keep from knowing.
No, it is not whatever I think I know.
Maybe I'll never know whatever it is.
Some day it has to be figured out. Whatever.

somebody

Somebody's got to tell me the truth some day.
And if somebody doesn't tell me the truth I'll tell it.
On my block there was somebody knew the truth, I think.
Or so I thought. Anyway somebody knew
That trying to tell the truth is looking for somebody.

isn't

If it isn't anywhere I guess it isn't.
But if it isn't why do I think it is?
I guess there really isn't any way
For me to find out what is or isn't there
In the black night where it either was or wasn't.

where

Where was it I was looking in the past?
It isn't where I've looked, that's no surprise.
I don't know what or where it is or was.
But maybe it isn't so much the where but the why.
Or maybe I haven't found it because beware.

Name

I wish I could recall now the lines written across the surface of my dream. They said Name investigated the possibility of its own happiness muttering and frowning preoccupied so that it noticed nobody else at all though somehow you could tell that it knew somebody was standing there in the doorway looking in at it and watching what it was doing rummaging in desk drawers opening notebooks shutting them up again writing down something or other on a scrap of paper which would very soon be carelessly thrown away in a wastebasket and go off in the trash somewhere out of the city burning stinking unrecoverable though like memory not biodegradable.

A Thank-You Note

– for Richard and Charlee Wilbur

As with the skill of verses properly managed
The little river quietly makes its way
Along the valley and through the local village
Below the smiling hospitable house,
Easily flowing over the shining stones,
Trochee, and anapest, pyrrhic, and also spondee,
Under the heartbeat easy governance
Of long continued metrical discipline.

Its fields and woods in their good order are
A figure for the manners of that house,
Disposed for intelligent pleasure, and for welcome.

Of Rhyme

The task is the discovering of a rhyme
Whose consequence is just though unforeknown
Either in its completion having been
Prepared for though in secret all the time

Or in the way each step of the way brings in
To play with one another in the game
Considerations hitherto unknown,
New differences discovering the same.

The discovering is an ordering in time
Such that one seems to chance upon one's own
Birth name strangely engraved upon a stone
In consequence of the completion of the rhyme.

Measure 100

There is a passage in the Mozart K.
511 Rondo in A Minor,

Measures 98 through 101,
And focused on measure 100, where there are

At least four different melodies, or fragments
Of melodies, together and apart,

Resolving themselves, or unresolving themselves
With: enigmatic sweetness, or melancholy;

Distant memories of victories,
Personal, royal, or mythic over demons;

Sophisticated talking about ideas;
Moments of social or sexual concord; or

Of parting though with mutual regret;
Differences and likenesses of natures;

It was what you said last night, whoever you are,
That told me what your nature is, and didn't;

It was the way you said the things that you said,
Grammar and syntax, agents of our fate;

Allusions to disappointments; as also
To an unexpected gift somebody gave

To someone there in the room behind the music;
Someone else working out a problem

At a table under the glowing light of a lamp;
Or the moment when the disease has finally

Proceeded to its foregone working through,
Leaving behind it nothing but the question

Of whether there's a heaven to sing about.
The clarity and poise of the arrangement,

The confidence in the very writing of it
Fosters the erroneous impression that

There's all the truth there is, in the little nexus,
Encapsulated here in narratives

Diminutive in form, perfectly told,
As far as they are willing to be told.

According to the dictionary, "resolve"
Derives from "solve" and "solve" derives from the Latin

"Solvere" that means "untie," and "re-"
Is an intensifier, meaning "again,"

And so, again, again, and again, what's tied
Must be untied again, and again, and again;

Or else it's like what happens inside a lock,
The cylinders moving back and forth as the lock

Is locked, unlocked, and locked, over and over.

Rereading Old Writing

Looking back, the language scribbles.
What's hidden, having been said?
Almost everything? Thrilling to think
There was a secret there somewhere,
A bird singing in the heart's forest.

Two people sitting by a river;
Sunlight, shadow, some pretty trees;
Death dappling in the flowing water;
Beautiful to think about,
Romance inscrutable as music.

Out of the ground, in New Jersey, my mother's
Voice, toneless, wailing – beseeching?
Crying out nothing? A winter vapor,
Out of the urn, rising in the yellow
Air, an ashy smear on the page.

The quiet room floats on the waters,
Buoyed up gently on the daylight;
The branch I can see stirs a little;
Nothing to think about; writing
Is a way of being happy.

What's going to be in this place?
A person entering a room?
Saying something? Signaling?
Writing a formula on a blackboard.
Something not to be understood.

Learning from History

They said, my saints, my slogan-sayers sang,
Be good, my child, in spite of all alarm.
They stood, my fathers, tall in a row and said,
Be good, be brave, you shall not come to harm.

I heard them in my sleep and muttering dream
And murmuring cried, How shall I wake to this?
They said, my poets, singers of my song,
We cannot tell, since all we tell you is

But history, we speak but of the dead.
And of the dead they said such history
(Their beards were blazing with the truth of it)
As made of much of me a mystery.

As in my covered sleep I dreamt of waking,
I dreamed that I went solitary roving
Over the sunk cities of my ancestors,
Over a darkness, over a deepness swimming.

Dreaming of this I was when they spoke to me.
Lovers they bragged of, long since dead and gone,
Whose ashes through the ages of their death
Patiently break. Long since are they gone.

They said, my sages, my truth tellers told
Tall tales of captains gone into their graves.
How pitiful they fell that had been bold!
The little that they tell is, history saves

Little, and what it saves is hardly told,
And what is hardly told is hardly heard.
Something repeats, they say. Of what it is
Or how be told, these captains have no word.

Now they are sunk under the wave of earth.
Down there their cries are faint and tiny and
Their phantom chariots and their phantom horses
Stand transfixed in the landscape of their death.

An die Parzen

– Hölderlin

Give me, O You who have the power to do so,
But one summer more, and the autumn following after,
To bring my songs to harvest. And then my heart,
Satisfied with its playing, may willingly die.

The soul that never finished the work for which
It came into this world will never rest easy
Down there with Orcus; but if the work gets done,
Then I will unprotestingly go down

Into the stillness of the world of shadows.
What if I cannot carry my lyre with me? –
One time, at least, I lived as the gods live.
Nothing more than this was necessary.

In the Reading Room

Alone in the library room, even when others
Are there in the room, alone, except for themselves;
There is the illusion of peace; the air in the room

Is stilled; there are reading lights on the tables,
Looking as if they're reading, looking as if
They're studying the text, and understanding,

Shedding light on what the words are saying;
But under their steady imbecile gaze the page
Is blank, patiently waiting not to be blank.

The page is blank until the mind that reads
Crosses the black river, seeking the Queen
Of the Underworld, Persephone. where she sits

By the side of the one who brought her there from Enna,
Hades the mute, the deaf, king of the dead letter;
She is clothed in the beautiful garment of our thousand

Misunderstandings of the sacred text.

I

Spring

– from Virgil, Georgics, II, ii. 323-345

It's spring that adorns the woods and groves with leaves;
In spring the soil, desiring seed, is tumid,
And then the omnipotent father god descends
In showers from the sky and enters into
The joyful bridal body of the earth,
His greatness and her greatness in their union,
Bringing to life the life waiting to live.
Birdsong is heard in every secluded thicket,
And all the beasts of the field have become aware
That love's appointed days have come again.
The generous earth is ready to give birth
And the meadows ungirdle for Zephyr's warming breezes;
The tender dew is there on everything;
The new grass dares entrust itself to the new
Suns of the new days and the little tendrils
Of the young vines have no fear of a South Wind coming
Nor of a North Wind from a stormy sky;
The vine brings forth its buds; its leaves unfold.
I think it must have been that just such days
As these were the shining days when the world was new;
Everywhere it was spring, the whole world over;
The East Wind held in check its winter winds;
The beasts drank in the light of that first dawn;
The first men, born of the earth, raised up their heads
From the stony ground; the woods were stocked with game,
And the first stars came out in the sky above.
Nor could the tender plants endure their lot
If spring's relief were not to intervene
Between the heat of summer and winter's cold.

Levis Exsurgit Zephirus

– Goliardic

The wind stirs lightly as the sun's
Warmth stirs in the new season's
Moment when the earth shows everything
She has, her fragrance on everything.

The spring royally in his excitement
Scatters the new season's commandment
Everywhere, and the new leaves open,
The buds open, and begin to happen.

The winged and the fourfooted creatures
According to their several natures
Find or build their nesting places;
Each unknowingly rejoices.

Held apart from the season's pleasure
According to my separate nature,
Nevertheless I bless and praise
The new beginning of the new days,

Seeing it all, hearing it all,
The leaf opening, the first bird call

Descriptive

Alone, I looked down through the afternoon:
A long lawn, a great tree, a field, and a fountain.
The whole day was full of its colors that moved
About, above, within, and of each other.

The whole day was alive with its own creating.
Nothing was still, would stay, and for a while
I looked at all this as if it were all I wanted,
Colors and shapes, fluid as one another,

So that the tree, which seemed at one moment a tree,
Seemed at another an inexhaustible fountain
Cascading about itself in a green fall
Of water that never fell, and the green lawn

Was the water that never fell, running away.

The Bird

Minding of itself, and mildly, in its finding,
And modestly, submissive to the weather,

Storm, wind, the birds' peril, this bird I saw
That did not see me in my human body watching.

Watchful the bird was only of itself,
And listening to itself, with softliest mutter,

And twitter, and quietest fluttering of feather,
Attentive to the minutiae of its task.

.

The Beach at Evening

The beach at this evening full-
Tide is a fisherman's back,
Whose bright muscles of rock
Glisten and strain as they pull

The cast net of the sea
In with a full catch
Of pebble, shell, and other
Things that belong to the sea.

Dialogue

the mind

I am that thing the sea cast up, a shell
Within whose murmuring sound the tide or wind
Murmur their old music. My coil is cunning,
Envy, malice, pity, contemplation ...
The wave that cast me out upon this beach
An hour ago, where I sit singing alone,
Will lace me round with her green arms, come tide,
Come evening, and I will be gone. Meanwhile
I hum to myself myself in a humming dream.

the body

I am that sea. What I cast up is mine,
Whenever I choose to take it back or not.
The driest bloom that spreads its papery petal
Far inland bears my legend on its flowering.
Read my sign in the lizard's grin. My voice
Cries out in the falling flesh of the great Bathsheba.
The little dog that leaps up in the field
Leaps up as if to leap out of my reach.
But I will wash him down. And thou, my mind.

The Embarkation for Cythera

The picnic-goers beautified themselves
And then set sail for Cythera, with jugs
To keep their coffee hot, martinis cold,
And hampers full of music. The water shone
For them that day, and like a street of jewels
Lay between their land and the island.

Their cockle hull was pretty, white and gold
As the Mozarteum, and their laughter picked
Its way, with implicating melody,
From port to starboard, gentlemen to ladies
And return. They played their cards right, whiling
The day away by smiling and by thinking

Of the times to come, the banquets in the grove
On the antless island of that ancient idol
Love, the girl who rose to be the pearl
To deck them out. Thinking of her, each lady
Fingered her necklace, and sweet music tattled
From the spinet of her desire; each lord

Touched at his sleeve for the ace he'd hidden there.

Cythera

There they go, down to the fatal ship.
They know how beautiful they are.
The ship will sail very soon. The sea
Will cover them over very soon unknowingly.

Wave goodbye from the shore, children.
I can see how your faces change in the sight
Of their going away. Wave to them.

Their sails are of silk, they're very pretty.
The sunset is all smiles, radiance,
The hues of a first, or last, innocence.
You look hungry, children, tired, angry.

Very beautiful is the manner of their going:
Music is playing about the mast; their lovely faces
Look lovelier still compared to the angry children.

Down by the River

The page is green. Like water words are drifting
Across the notebook page on a day in June
Of irresistible good weather. Everything's easy.

On this side of the river, on a bench near the water,
A young man is peaceably stroking the arm of a girl.
He is dreaming of eating a peach. Somebody's rowing,

Somebody's running, over the bridge that goes over
The highway beyond the river. The river is blue,
The river is moving along, taking it easy.

A breeze has come up, and somewhere a dog is barking,
Acknowledging the stirring of the breeze.
Nobody knows whose dog. The river is moving,

The boats are moving with it or else against it.
People beside the river are watching the boats.
Along the pathway on this side of the river

Somebody's running, looking good in the sunshine,
Everything going along with everything else,
Moving along in participial rhythm,

Flowing, enjoying, taking its own sweet time.
On the other side of the river somebody else,
A man or a woman, is painting the scene I'm part of.

A brilliantly clear diminutive figure works
At a tiny easel, and as a result my soul
Lives on forever in somebody's heavenly picture.

Out at Lanesville

– i.m. Mary Ann Youngren, 1932-1980

The five or six of them, sitting on the rocks
Out at Lanesville, near Gloucester. It is like
Listening to music. Several of them are teachers,
One is a psychologist, one is reading a book,
The page glares white in the summer sunlight;
Others are just sunning themselves, or just
Sitting there looking out over the water;
A couple of them seem to be talking together;
From this far off you can't hear what they are saying.

The day is hot, the absolute middle of summer.
Someone has written an obscenity
In huge letters on the rocks above and behind
This group of people, and someone else, one of them,
Maybe, or maybe a neighbor, the owner of one
Of the cottages up behind and back in the woods,
Has tried to erase it and only partly done so,
So that for years it will say hoarsely FUCK
To the random winds and to the senseless waves.

One of them is sitting with her back turned
To me and to the others on the rocks. The purple
Loosestrife and the tigerlilies are like the flags
Of some celebration; they bloom along the edge
Of a small stream that makes its way unseen
Down to the rocks and sand. Her shoulders are round,
And rather luxuriously heavy, and the whole figure
Has a youthful and graceful amplitude of being
Whose beauty will last her her whole life long.

The voices of some people out in a boat somewhere
Are carried in over the water with surprising
Force and clarity, though saying I don't know what:
Happiness; unhappiness; something about the conditions
Of all such things; work done, not done; the saving

Of the self in the intense work of its singleness,
Learning to live with it. Their lives have separate ends.
Suddenly she turns her head and seems to look
Towards me and towards the others on the rocks,

So that her body, turned away, is more expressive
Than her blank face, a pure reflector of the light.

La Farandola dei Fanciulli

– Montale

How far back the ancient past seems now.
Those kids dancing around and playing,
By the railroad track, up back of the beach,
On the gravel and cinders of the railbed,

Weeds suddenly breaking into blossom
In the heat of the day, a flowering of thirst.
It's as if being naked and nameless
Was being sunlight, flower, heat-shimmer.

The Crippled Girl, The Rose

It was as if a flower bloomed as if
Its muttering root and stem had suddenly spoken,

Uttering on the air a poem of summer,
The rose the utterance of its root and stem.

Thus her beautiful face, the crippled girl's,
Was like the poem spoken by her body.

Roof

Four or five men on the high roof
Of the apartment house I see from out my window,

Angels or other beings from an element
Other than ours but similar although

Superior so bright and clear, perfected
In diminutive particular; angels

Or little brilliant demons or simian
Creatures with nose-and-mouth mask snouts

Against the fumes of the material
A tiny glittering machine is putting down.

The fumes are visible and drift away,
Like martyred souls made visible in the radiant air.

Harvesters Resting

– after Millet

In the middle of the day, in the great shadow
Of the grainstack, the harvesters
Are resting and having their midday meal.

Boaz is approaching with a woman.
Meticulous as cattle in their attention
To the task of resting and feeding,

Some of them seem not to have noticed.
Others regard her with the slow,
Blind, thorough look that cattle have,

Spellbound in the noontime heat.

A Morning Song

A bird cried out among the first things of the morning.
I dreamed about murders all night long.

The stone changed color among the shadows as the sun came up.
It was the bird's cry that startled up the stone.

Horses

– for Tom Sleigh

It is true that, as he said, the horses,
When the lightning signaled something
Along the horizon, acknowledged the signaling,

Moving about in extraordinary beauty
Of shifting and neighing, flicker of ear,
Changings of pace, slidings, turnings,

The delicate legs finding out something
The ground could tell them, interpreting
The sky's statement of oncoming darkness.

The storm was doing whatever it does,
Matrix of signaling, along the horizon.
In the valley the houses were brilliantly

Clear, the storm's darkness was making
Possible a perfect delineation,
The houses' edges brimming with light.

Unos Caballos

– Jorge Guillén

There are several horses grazing in the field,
Motionless almost, untroubled as the grass

Silently growing there in the light of the natural
Morning before the beginning of anything human.

Docile in the confines of the pasture
These hairy, unyoked, idle, quiet creatures

In vegetative peacefulness show no sign
Of understanding. Their shadowed eyes and tranquil

Ears know nothing of the vigil that they keep.
The serenity of heaven is realized

In their obliviousness of it, grazing there.

In Balance

– Jorge Guillén

I am so happy. It is wonderful
To breathe the air and be in the morning light.
On a day like this, if the soul weighs anything
It is like the weight of a flower bending itself
Down to the earth in the weightless light and air.

Everything calmly gives itself up
To happiness on a day like this. The whiteness
Of a wall gives whiteness to the eye that looks at it.
The grass in the vacant lot across the street
Yields to the morning breeze that flows across it,

Till the breeze dies down like the end of a sentence spoken.

Hälfte des Lebens

– Hölderlin

The yellow pear tree boughs
And the wild rose branches hanging
Over the quiet waters;

And the swans, a little drunken,
Kiss, and kiss again
The sacred summer waters.

Alas, when winter comes,
Where will I find such flowers?
Where will I find the sunlight

And shadows of the summer?
The walls are speechless, cold;
The weather vane bangs in the wind.

When We Were Children

– "der Wilde Alexander" (fl. late 13th C.)

I remember how, at that time, in this meadow,
We used to run up and down, playing our games,
Tag and games of that sort; and looked for wildflowers,
Violets and such. A long time ago.
Now there are only these cows, bothered by flies,
Only these cows, wandering about in the meadow.

I remember us sitting down in the field of flowers,
Surrounded by flowers, and playing she loves me not,
She loves me; plucking the flower petals.
My memory of childhood is full of those flowers,
Bright with the colors of garlands we wore in our dancing
And playing. So time went by among the wildflowers.

Look over there near those trees at the edge of the woods.
Right over there is where we used to find
Blueberry bushes, blackberry bushes, wild strawberries.
We had to climb over rocks and old walls to get them.
One day a man called out to us: "Children, go home."
He had been watching from somewhere in the woods.

We used to feast on the berries we found in that place
Till our hands and mouths were stained with the colors of all
The berries, the blackberries, strawberries, and the blueberries.
It was all fun to us, in the days of our childhood.
One day a man called out, in a doleful voice:
"Go home, children, go home, there are snakes in that place."

One day one of the children went into the grass
That grows high near the woods, among the bushes.
We heard him scream and cry out. He came back weeping.
"Our little horse is lying down and bleeding.
Our pony is lying down. Our pony is dying.
I saw a snake go crawling off in the grass."

Children, go home, before it gets too dark.
If you don't go home before the light has gone,
If you don't get home before the night has come,
Listen to me, you will be lost in the dark,
Listen to me, your joy will turn into sorrow.
Children, go home, before it gets to be dark.

There were five virgins lingered in a field.
The king went in with his bride and shut the doors.
The palace doors were shut against the virgins.
The virgins wept, left standing in the field.
The servants came and stripped the virgins naked.
The virgins wept, stripped naked, in the field.

II

Roman Elegy VIII

– Goethe

When you tell me that you were unpopular as a child,
And that your mother spoke of you in a rueful

Tone of voice, and that all this seemed to go on
For a very long time, the slow time that it took

For you to grow up, I believe you, and I enjoy
Thinking about that odd, awkward child.

The grapevine-flower, you know, is nothing much,
But the ripened fruit gives pleasure to men and gods.

The Lesson

– from the Latin of Samuel Johnson

The stream still flows through the meadow grass,
As clear as it was when I used to go in swimming,
Not good at it at all, while my father's voice
Gently called out through the light of the shadowy glade,
Trying to help me learn. The branches hung down low
Over those waters made secret by their shadows.
My arms flailed in a childlike helpless way.

And now the sharp blade of the axe of time
Has utterly cut away that tangle of shadows.
The naked waters are open to the sky now
And the stream still flows through the meadow grass.

Poem

– i.m. GEF Jr.

The ancient cup of tears, the pastoral legend,
Hid in the wood from which we've long since strayed,
Darkest of clearest pools, in whose reflection,
Or magnified, or simplified, perfected,
The motions of our childhood lost were held
Or moving in the motion of the slight
Rippling as the light wind fled across it,
Is it the pool in which we cannot look now
Nor drink from the dark freshness of that source
From which the pure words sprang that could be spoken
To utter a sorrow impersonal as legend?

In the Garden

The impatiens in the tub, beside the wooden bench
I'm sitting on, has leaves that are uniformly
A light green almost to the state of water,
Different from the impatiens twenty feet away,
Over by the birdbath. Are they a different
Species or are the differences the result
Of different conditions of light or earth?
The green of these leaves is almost an absence of green,
And the stalks look like rays of light under water.

The blossoms are pure white, with yellow centers.
I just this minute noticed that there are yellow
Five-petalled flowers blooming in the little
Patch of clover in the ground beside the tub.
These yellow flowers have centers of a paler
Yellow growing out of a tender matrix
Of green; and growing out of the same stalk
Is a pod shaped like a little zucchini, or steeple,
Pointed, tall by comparison with the flowers.

There is something springlike and free about the littleness,
Oddness, and lightness of this combination of things,
Observed here at the very tag end of summer,
In my good fortune. Another little plant,
A weed I also don't know the name of,
With a white flower shaped like a deep cup,
And with blue-tipped sexual parts, lies in the grass,
The fallen maiden of some casual violence.
The whole plucked stalk is an event in time:

A number of blossoms one above the other,
But some blossoms more fully out than others,
In an intricately regular scale or series.
Of course, since the flower is plucked, it isn't really
An event in time, but only the record of an event.
Now there are a few leaves falling from the ash tree

In the Garden

In the steady mild wind. What's to come of all this
Ill-informed staring at little flowers and
Enigmatic misleading stalks and leaves?

It isn't autumn yet. There will be late autumn flowers.
When the wind started up suddenly just now,
When I was sitting in the garden reading Edward Thomas,
When I was looking at the back wall of our house,
Soon to be different after the new porch is built,
When I had just had lunch with a friend who spoke
Of how she used to be a lush and now
Eats no meat, no sugar, and no dairy,
When my daughter in another part of the garden

Was reading *The Mayor of Casterbridge*, and the branches
Of the white fringe and the witch hazel shifted
Suddenly, horizontally, and other branches
In the garden suddenly stirred and shifted, it was
As if these trees and bushes, the white ash, the sugar-
Maple, the deutzia, the young unflowering pear tree,
Had all suddenly had the same idea,
Of motion and quiet sound and the changing light,
A subtle, brilliant, and a shadowy idea.

A Young Woman

That she, with such gifts given,
In the abundance and grace

Of her youth and sweetness,
As if in a garden, walking,

In a summer of freshness
And of the wind lifting

And falling in a lavishing
Of light and penultimate

Shadow, that she should falter
At all through this phase,

Pressing, with hand outstretched,
The surface of the future,

As one who is blind presses
The surface of darkness,

Of corridor, or wall,
For any assurance at all,

May she be blessed
In this faltering forward.

Goodnight

Lying in bed and waiting to find out
Whatever is going to happen: the windowshade

Making its slightest sound as the night wind,
Outside, in the night, breathes quietly on it;

It is parental hovering over the infantile;
Something like that; it is like being a baby,

And over the sleep of the baby there is a father,
Or mother, breathing, hovering; the streetlight light

In the nighttime branches breathing quietly too;
Altering; realtering; it is the body breathing;

The crib of knowing: something about what the day
Will bring; and something about what the night will hold,

Safely, at least for the rest of the night, I pray.

Abyss

– Baudelaire, "Le Gouffre"

Pascal's abyss was with him everywhere.
Everything is an abyss. Anything
That is done; that happens; is thought; is put into words.

I can't begin to tell you how many times
The fear in the sound of the wind has made my skin creep.
The deep; the long white empty beach stretching on

For ever; the silence; the desire of falling.
God has written out something on the face of the dark
In a hand absolutely sure of what it is doing.

I am afraid of sleep because I am afraid
Of a hole empty with horror. I can see nothing
Out of my window but infinity.

My acrophobic spirit is falling in love –
To be nowhere! – free of being, form, and name!

Nocturnal

It is always among sleepers we walk.
We walk in their dreams. None of us
Knows what he is as he walks
In the dream of another. *Tell me my name.*
Your tongue is blurred, honeyed with error.
Your sleep's truth murmurs its secret.

Tell me your name. Out at the edge,
Out in the cold, out in the cold
That came into the house in your clothes
The wind's hands hold on to nothing,
Moaning, over the edge of the cliff,
The wind babble unintelligible.

A Night-Time River Road

We were driving down a road.
Where was it we were going?
Where were we driving to?
Nobody knew.

Behind the blur of trees
Along the river road,
Somewhere behind the blur
A dark river ran.

The car bore us along.
We didn't know who we were
Or where we were going to.
Somebody must know.

Somebody in the car
Must know where we were going,
Where we were going to,
Beside the dark river.

All silent in the car
We sat staring ahead.
Where were the lights of a bar,
A gas station, a house?

Out in the dark the river
Was telling itself a story.
There in the car nobody
Could tell where we were going.

Caprimulgidae

It makes its flight in the competence of its own
Way of behaving; hovering, or gliding,
Floating, oddly, just at the edges of bushes,
Just over the ground, or near the vagueness of trees,
At twilight, on the hunt for moths or other
Creatures out in the failing evening light.
It feeds while flying softly, smiling, smiling,
The gape open to far back under the ears;
In the dim air it looks like a giant moth
Fluttering, the blurred disheveled feathers waving,
Signaling something that understands its meaning.

Its young are born unhelpless. Caprimulgus
Can totter or hop only a few steps,
Almost a cripple, its little legs so feeble;
Perhaps on the flat roof of some city building,
Or out on the bare ground, or along a limb,
It lies all day, waking in its sleeping;
Capable, safe, concealed in its cryptic plumage,
Invisible to almost anything;
Its nightready eyes are closed, carefully
Keeping the brilliant secret of its flight;
Its hunting begins when the light begins to go.

At the Bus Stop; Eurydice

The old lady's face.
Who knows whose it was?
The bus slid by me.
Who in the world knows me?

She was amazed, amazed.
Can death really take me?
The bus went away.
It took the old lady away.

Ellery Street

How much too eloquent are the songs we sing:
Nothing we tell will tell how beautiful is the body.

It does not belong
Even to him or her who lives in it.

Beautiful the snail's body which it bears
Laboriously in its way through the long garden.

The old lady who lives next door has terribly scarred legs.
She bears her body laboriously to the Laundromat.

There's a fat girl in the apartment across the street.
I can see her unhappiness in the flower she wears

In her hair; it blooms in her hair like a flower
In a garden, like a flower flowering in a dream

Dreamed all night, a night-
Blooming flower. A boy passes by, his bare

Chest flashing like a shield in the summer air;
All-conquering,

The king, going to the drug store.
The snail crosses the garden in its dignified silence.

Street Scene

Someone's shadow and the shadow of his dog
Are what I see through my window looking out
Across the street. Someone's shadow, and then
As the leaves of the tree just outside my window
Move a little, this way, or that, with the breeze,
It's Mr.Wrenn, taking his dog for a walk,
Or being out there with his dog, in order, maybe,
To be seen as one of us; the two of them,
Standing there, vacant of conversation;
His tan shirt, brown pants, bald spot, his trivial pug
Absurdly the color of a golden retriever.

That this huge stage presenteth nought but shows

The red truck that was parked in the parking lot
That they have walked past without seeming to notice it,
Is now leaving the parking lot. It is as if
The man and his dog, both of them, knew that the truck
Was going to move, because all three of them have
Become, in common, elements of the scene
That I'm observing and so all three of them seem
To understand that they have a common purpose.
The side of the red truck just a moment ago
Had, painted on it in white graphics, CHARETTE.
That word was on it when it left my view.
Now, a blue truck with no letters on its side,
So giving no information about its purpose,
Turns into the parking lot and then backs into
The same slot under the overhang of the building.
A shifting of the leaves that I'm looking through
Prevents me from seeing who gets out of the truck
And where it is he goes. It is as if
The brilliant red truck with the white letters on it,
Outside my range of sight had changed its color,

Whereon, by day, the stars in secret comment,

And therefore it is as if I had imagined
The change of color, the vanishing of the one truck,
The sudden appearance of the other one.
Magic. A trick of magic performed by me,
Something that I performed because I saw it.
Or the trick was performed by the unseen hand of the world.
CHARETTE went out of business in that instant.
And what became of Mr. Wrenn and his dog?
Hurled down to the Underworld, twisting and turning,
The two of them falling, the dog's leash fluttering
In the eerie light down there through which they fall.

Courtesy

It is an afternoon towards the end of August:
Autumnal weather, cool following on,
And riding in, after the heat of summer,
Into the empty afternoon shade and light,

The shade full of light without any thickness at all;
You can see right through and right down into the depth
Of the light and shade of the afternoon; there isn't
Any weight of the summer pressing down.

In the backyard of the house next door there's a kid,
Maybe eleven or twelve, and a young man,
Visitors at the house whom I don't know,
The house in which the sound of some kind of party,

Perhaps even a wedding, is going on.
Somehow you can tell from the tone of their voices
That they don't know each other very well –
Two guests at the party, one of them, maybe,

A friend of the bride or groom, the other the son
Or the younger brother, maybe, of somebody there.
A couple of blocks away the wash of traffic
Dimly sounds, as if we were near the ocean.

They're shooting baskets, amiably and mildly.
The noise of the basketball, though startlingly louder
Than the voices of the two of them as they play,
Is peaceable as can be, something like meter.

The earnest voice of the kid, girlish and manly;
And the voice of the young man, carefully playing the game
Of having a grown up conversation with him.
I can tell the young man is teaching the boy by example,

Courtesy

The easy way he dribbles the ball and passes it
Back with a single gesture of wrist to make it
Easy for the kid to be in synch;
Giving and taking, perfectly understood.

Herbsttag

– Rilke

Now is the right time, Lord. Summer is over.
Let the autumn shadows drift upon the sundials,
And let the wind stray loose over the fields.

Summer was abundant. May the last fruits be full
Of its promise. Give them a last few summer days.
Bring everything into its completion, Lord,
The last sweetness final in the heavy wine.

Who has no house will never have one now;
Who is alone will spend his days alone;
Will wake to read some pages of a book;
Will write long letters; wander unpeacefully,
Late in the night, in the streets, while the leaves stray down.

My Harvest

– from Hölderlin, "Mein Eigentum"

The autumn day is quiet in its fullness.
The grapes are ripe, and the hedges red with berries;
Already many beautiful blossoms have fallen
Gratefully down to the earth to be received.

And as I make my way along the path
I see how men are laboring in contentment
Over there in the fields, because their work
Has ripened into a harvest of good fortune.

October

The day was hot, and entirely breathless, so
The remarkably quiet, remarkably steady leaf fall
Seemed as if it had no cause at all.

The ticking sound of falling leaves was like
The ticking sound of gentle rainfall as
They gently fell on leaves already fallen

Or as, when as they passed them in their falling,
Now and again it happened that one of them touched
One or another leaf as yet not falling,

Still clinging to the idea of being summer:
As if the leaves that were falling but not the day,
Had read, and understood, the calendar.

An Autumn Afternoon

The rich fume of autumn rises from the ground
In light and odor as the leaves rot marvelously

In the hot autumn sun. In the autumn afternoon
What was green is turning to light before my eyes.

The hawthorn leaves have not yet fallen away.
The squirrels are fat. The winter is coming soon.

There's something frantic in birdflight. The shadows of wings
Print and unprint erratically on the little

Porch roof that I look out on from my window,
As if to keep taking back what has just been said.

Autumn

– Rilke, "Herbst"

The autumn leaves are falling,
Falling as if from far

Heavenly groves whose leaves
Are gesturing as they fall,

Hands protesting their falling.
The earth is falling too,

Falling through the night
Among indifferent stars.

See, this hand is falling.
All of us are falling.

It is in everything.
(Yet there is One who holds

Carefully in his hand
Everything falling forever.)

Out in the Cold

The sun shines in the ice of my country
As my smile glitters in the mirror of my devotion.
Flat is the scene there. There are a few scrub bushes.
I live on the edge of the land. The frozen sea
Lies locked for a thousand miles to the North, to the Pole.

Meager my mouth, and my knuckles sharp and white.
They will hurt when I hit. I fish for a fish
So thin and sharp in the tooth as to suit my malice.
It stares like any fish. But it knows a lot,
Knows what I know. Astonishment it has not.

I have a hut to which I go at night.
Sometimes there is no night, and the midnight sun
And I sit up all night and fish for that fish.
We huddle over the ice, the two of us.

A Farewell

Let the day fall like light out of the eye.
Out of the ear let its music go. From the touch
Let the touching of air retire. Remain in the dark,
Dumbly remain in the dark. What will they know
Of you then, or want, when, then, in the dark you remain?

Knowledge began with the pressure of light on the eye,
And the ear spun out of thin air its airy tune.
Let no vein flutter or flicker to signal the blood's
All but imperceptible errand. Does the skin
Shudder or shiver at all at least conjunction?

Shrink, then, into your dark, be locked up in yourself,
Shadow of shadow be in your nothing dark,
Oh be keep to yourself, be close, be moat, be wall
All dark. Hush. Hear hush. Vanish. Know nothing.
How then will the day light knock at the lid in vain!

In the Dark

I wandered in my mind as in the dark.
I stumbled over a chair, ran into a wall,
Or another wall, I wandered down a hall,
And into another room, the same as before.
I stumbled against a wall, I felt the floor
Carefully with each foot, I found a door,
And into another room, the same as before.
I wandered in my mind, I was in the dark.
I sidled up against another wall,
I shouldered along it, searching for a door,
And found one, opening out into a hall
That led to another room, the same as before.
In fear I tuned my voice to a little tune,
A crazy tune that sang inside my head,
And followed the tune as one would follow a thread
That leads one to or from a minotaur.
And that tune led me back or forward mazily,
That sang inside my head so crazily!

I followed or fled at last into a hall
That had a little light. Down at the end
Of the hall, a long way off, two windows were,
And into the windows came a little light.
I followed down the hall as to a friend
Long since offended. Timidly I wore
An anxious smile, eager to please. The light
Grew brighter still, till at last to the end
Of the hall I came. What a wonderful sight!
I found that I was looking through my eyes!
Outside of my self the ordinary day light was!

Janus

– adapted from Ovid, Fasti. *I, 95-120.*

My house filled up with light in the midnight dark.
The headlights swiveled against me, swiveled and yawed.
It was the blind two-headed god looking at me.
My hair stood up on end. Cold terror froze my chest.

Noise and confusion. "Chaos was my name
When the ancients named me. There was a time when earth,
Air, fire, and water were clotted together, all
One inchoate lump; and then they four

In discord separated, one from the other.
Fire went up higher than all the others;
Air intervened between the fire above,
And earth, below, and sea below the earth,

Each of them in its place, although uneasy.
All things are what I govern, just at that moment
When out of nothing they turn into something.
And Janus is the ore and residue."

Garden Dog

In the winter, out in the winter
sunlight, watched from the upstairs

window, by the binocular eye,
out in the winter light

the dog is wandering, sniffing
for enemies burrowed in Ireland

sometime in the nineteenth century.
What's in a dog's heart ?

The terrier brown coat
touched into orange flame,

blue, purple, pink,
by the binocular gaze,

the brilliant monster is wandering,
smelling the winter air.

The wind is light. The light
is wandering, blown by the breezes.

What's in the way the sun shines down?
Sniffing the sticks and stones,

sniffing the dirt and dormant
unflourishing grass in the garden,

out in the winter light.

Backyard Dog

Out in the winter moonlight,
Out in the cold snow,
The dog is running around

Around and around and around
In the fenced-in backyard,
In spirals ignited by

The binocular's wondering gaze,
Magical dogtracks out
In the cold winter moonlight,

The dogtracks spiraling
Around and around, a soul,
A saying, a writing being

Written over and over,
Written and rewritten
In the newly fallen snow.

First Night

– "Janus was not yet an anthropomorphized god"

A stump. A post. An effigy not made
As yet. A toe. A toe in the icy waters.

A door that's open just a little.
What's that in the next room?

What flows underneath our house?
Timor mortis conturbat me.

*

First night. Absence of light. Presence
Of cold. Numb fingers play the instruments.

Down in the street a little horn is tooting.
Cold fog in the throat.

Trying to clear the throat, a new beginning.
Timor mortis conturbat me.

*

The year turns over heavily in its sleep.
The whole sky wheels above the starry treetop

That is the sleeping city's dreaming head.
If I should die before I wake

I pray the Lord my soul to take.
Timor mortis conturbat me.

The Chair

The chair left out in the garden night all winter
Sits waiting for the summer day all night.

The insides of the metal arms are frozen.
Over the house the night sky wheels and turns

All winter long even behind the day.

III

Your Personal God

– from Horace, Epistle *ii. 2, ll. 180 -189*

Jewels, marble, ivory, paintings, beautiful Tuscan
Pottery, silver, Gaetulian robes dyed purple –
Many there are who'd love to have all of these things.
There are some who don't care about them in the least.
Why one twin brother lives for nothing but pleasure,
And loves to fool around even more than Herod
Loves his abundant gardens of date-trees, while
The other twin brother works from morning to night
Improving his farm, ploughing and clearing the lands,
Pruning and planting, working his ass off, only
The genius knows, the personal god who knows
And controls the birth star of every person
There is in the world. Your personal god is the god
Who dies in a sense when your own breath gives out,
And yet lives on, after you die, to be
The personal god of somebody other than you;
Your personal god, whose countenance changes as
He looks at you, smiling sometimes, sometimes not.

Mnemosyne

– Hölderlin, "Mnemosyne"

i

Flowers, streams, hills, meadows, valleys –
Everything beautiful praises the Lord,
In order to find out whether or not He is.

A wedding day is beautiful. Human arrangements,
The keeping of laws to shelter in, can break your heart.
He can change any or all of it just as He pleases.
Law is nothing He needs of what we know of it.

The hero desires to be in that condition,
Where Truth *is* Being. The hero goes to the edge
And looks down over into whatever is there, or not,
In terror. God cannot do everything.
He cannot like the hero be in terror.

But everything is as it is, one way or another.
What does it all add up to, after all? Praise Him.

ii

Peaceful scene: the sunlight on the lawns;
The shadowy branches over the dry paths;
The smoke blossoming from the chimney tops;
The lark song almost lost in the perfect sky;
The sheep and cattle feeding in the fields,
Well-tended; the snow in the high meadows, flowering.

Value shining and flourishing everywhere.

Two people went this way, passing the cross
Once placed there long ago for the pious dead,
Two wanderers, one of them raging.

iii

Under the fig tree my Achilles lies,
Who died for me; and Ajax, near Scamander,
Under the sound of the wind, at the grotto's mouth,
In a foreign country, far from Salamis.

Heroes have died, in one way or another.

Some were astonished in the bloodsoaked field,
In the experience of their fate, surrounded;
Patroclus in the armor of his lover;
Others, in torment and bewilderment,
By their own hand, compelled to it by heaven.

Things go all wrong when He takes hold of one of us.
But everything is as it is, one way or another.

IV

Committee

Coldly the sun shone down on the moonlit scene.
Our committee stirred uneasily in its sleep.
Better not know too much too soon all about it.
The knees of grammar and syntax touched each other,
Furtive in pleasure under the oaken table.

The river lay not moving under the light
Of the shadowy earthly winter lunar scene.
The ends of justice are determined in
The conditions of our sleep. The spellbound scene
Arranged itself in a traditional way,

Transfixed and perfectly still. Unspoken agreements
Spoke volumes on the bookshelves of the room.

Trojan Horse

– Virgil, Aeneid, *II, ii. 250-264*

And now the heavens move and night comes in
And covers with its darkness earth and sky
And the tricks of the Myrmidons. Throughout the city
The Trojans, wearied by joy, lie fast asleep,
And now the Greeks set out from Tenedos,
Their ships in ordered formation, under the silent
Light of the friendly moon, making their way
Quietly towards the shore they know so well,
And when the lead ship's beacon light is shown,
Sinon, protected by the complicit fates,
Furtively opens up its wooden side,
And frees the Achaians from the Horse's womb.
The Horse releases them to the open air
And joyfully they come out. First come the captains
Thessander, and Sthenelus, and dire Ulysses,
Lowering themselves to the ground by means of a rope,
And Ácamas, Thoas, and Neoptólemus of
The house of Peleus, and Machaón the prince,
And Menelaus, and Epéus, he
Who built the Wooden Horse. They enter the city,
That slumbers submerged in wine and sleep; they surprise,
And quietly kill, the watchmen, and open the gates
To welcome in their comrades from the fleet,
Letting them in for what they are going to do.

Thermopylae

– Cavafy

Honor is due to those who are standing watch;
Sentinels guarding their own Thermopylae;
Never distracted from what's right to do,
And right to be; in all things virtuous,
But never so hardened by virtue as not to be

Compassionate, available to pity;
Generous if they're rich, but generous, too,
If they are poor, doing whatever they can;
Always true to the truth, no matter what,
But never scornful of those who have to lie.

Even more honor is due when, standing watch,
They see that the time will come when Ephialtes
Will tell the secret to the Medes and they
Will know the way to get in by the goat-path.

Evening News

We have been there
　　and seen nothing
Nothing has been there
　　for us to see

In what a beautiful distance
　　in the fresh dews
And morning lights
　　how radiantly

In the glistening
　　the village is wasted
It is by such sights
　　the eye is instructed

Little Vietnam Futurist Poem

She came into my view as vivid as
Somebody on a screen in a movie seen,
Elegant in the focus of my eye.

Bird-boned. Quick and light. Not wearing pyjamas.
The little run resembling playfulness.
Calling out something, screaming something or other

As if her little mouth was fervently singing,
As if you couldn't hear what the words could be,
Because of the singing. I had her in my sight.

Other people were there, wearing pajamas,
Streaming out of some hideyhole or other,
Into the way that that was how I saw them.

The trees of the kind that grew there establish the place.
We know that way the story of what it was.

What's Playing Tonight

Not twenty feet away were the walls of the house next door
    Where Bradley's mad mother and Bradley's sane father lived.

The shagbark hickory tree, absurdly tall, at night
    Loomed over the little houses, theirs and ours.

A movie kept on playing across the street on the screen
    That was the front of the house that was there asleep.

She didn't know how to run the movie projector, so
    She didn't know how to change the movie ever.

It played the same movie over and over again in the night.
    Pictures of dead Bradley still alive.

The neighborhood glowed with the flickering light of the silver screen
    That Bradley's mother's movie was playing on.

Evening News

The face looking into the room;
Behind it light, shaking, like heat
Lightning; the face calm and knowing;
Seeing, but not seeing who I am;
The mouth may be telling something.

Something about our helplessness;
Something about the confusions of beasts;
The consequence of error; systems
Haywire, or working; the stars gone
All wrong in the body's courses.

Out on the plain of Mars, brilliantly
Played under the lights, searched out
Beyond any answer, the game went on
Far into the night; the bloodiest came
Home from the battle seeking the prize.

The women were disgraced; hair streaming,
Pleading into the staring: buy, buy – ;
Was it the daughters I was seeing? –
The humiliation was pleasing: tears,
Laughter, smiles, all mingled together

The light swallowed itself, a balloon
Deflating; somewhere in the darkness
A murmuring let itself go.

On a Sunday Morning

My child and I
Are walking around the block.
No sea heaves near. No anger
Blooms through the perfect sky.

The flashing of the wheels
Of a passing car is not
The flashing of that fate
I might have feared, not this Sunday.

A page from a newspaper
Drifts along the gutter.
It is a leaf
Fallen from a terrible tree,

The tree of anger,
Tears, fearfulness.
It is nothing to him,
And nothing to me, this Sunday.

Virgil, *Aeneid*, II, ii. 705-744

"As he spoke we could hear, ever more loudly, the noise
Of the burning fires. The flood of flames was coming
Nearer and nearer.
           'My father, let me take you
Upon my shoulders and carry you with me.
The burden will be easy. Whatever happens,
You and I will experience it together,
Peril or safety, whichever it will be.
Little Iülus will come along beside me.
My wife will follow behind us. And you, my servants,
Listen to what I say: just as you leave
The limits of the city there is a mound,
And the vestiges of a deserted temple of Ceres,
And a cypress tree that has been preserved alive
For many years by the piety of our fathers.
We will all meet there, though perhaps by different ways
And, father, you must carry in your arms
The holy images of our household gods.
I, coming so late from the fighting and the carnage
Cannot presume to touch them until I have washed
Myself in running water.'
               Thus I spoke.
I take up the tawny pelt of a lion and
Cover my neck and my broad shoulders with it,
And bowing down, I accept the weight of my father;
Iülus puts his hand in mine and goes
Along beside me, trying to match my steps
As best he can, trying his best to keep up;
My wife follows behind us, at a distance.
So we all set out together, making our way
Among the shadows, and I, who only just
A little while ago had faced, undaunted,
Showers of arrows and swarms of enemy Greeks,
Am frightened by every slightest change in the air
And startled by every slightest sound I hear,
Fearful for whom I walk with and whom I carry.

And just as I had almost come to the gates
And thought that I had almost gotten us free,
I thought I heard the sound of many feet,
And my father, peering intently into the shadows,
Cries out to me, 'Get away, get away, my son,
My son, they are coming! I see their shining shields,
I see the glow of their weapons in the dark!'
I am alarmed, and I don't know what happened
But some power hostile to me distracts my wits,
And I am confused, and I lead us away by ways
That I don't know, and off the familiar streets
That together we are following, and so,
O God! some fate has taken away my wife,
Creusa, my wife, away from me. What happened?
Did she wander from the way that we were going?
Did she fall back, having to rest some place
Back there, and so we left her? I did not know.
I never saw her again, and as we went,
I never turned to look behind, and never
 Thought of her until we reached the mound
And Ceres' ancient place. When all of us,
At last, had gotten there, we all were there,
But she had vanished and she wasn't there.
Gone from her people, gone from her child, and her husband."

to where

Wearing a tawny lion pelt upon
My spindly shoulders I carry both of them,
My father and my mother, into the darkness,
My father hoarsely singing, "They are there!"
– The glimmer of something that is glimmering there –
"I see the glow of weapons in the shadows!"

Through which with my purblind eyes I think I see
Something in the darkness waiting there.
Above me in the dark my mother's voice
Calls down to me, "Who's there? Who is it there?"
Step after step together we make our way,
In the darkness of my memory of our house.

Sculptures by Dimitri Hadzi

This metal blooms in the dark of Rome's
Day light. Of how many deaths
Is Rome the bright flowering?
See, the dead bloom in the dark
Of the Fosse Ardeatina. The black
Breath of the war has breathed on them:
Shields gleam, and helmets, in the memory.

Their flowering is their being true
To their own nature; not being
A glory, a victory; being a record,
The way things are in war.
In the nature of things the flowers grow
With the authority of telling the truth:
Their brightness is dark with it.

What It Does

"Behold! here, where all that is to be seen
Is the smoke and dust that rises from the rubble
Of rocks piled upon rocks, there's Neptune, who
With his mighty trident brings down the walls and rears
The foundations up and with great surges heaves,
And upsets, and overturns the entire city."

Virgil, Aeneid, II, ii. 608-612, tr. David Ferry

The sea bit,
As they said it would,
And the hill slid,
As they said it would,
And the poor dead
Nodded agog
The poor head.

O topmost lofty
Tower of Troy,
The poem apparently
Speaks with joy
Of terrible things.
Where is the pleasure
The poetry brings?

Tell if you can,
What does it make?
A city of man
That will not shake,
Or if it shake,
Shake with the splendor
Of the poem's pleasure.

V

After Spotsylvania Court House

I read the brown sentences of my great-grandfather,
As if – not even as if, but actually –
Looking into a brown photograph as old
As his writing is. In his sentences
Two innocent naked young men, Methodists,
Bathe in the morning in the Rapahannock River,
At Fredericksburg, Virginia, eighteen sixty-four.
Brother Pierson and I went out and bathed in the Rapahannock,
Returned to take our breakfast on coffee and bread.
I can see the young men bathing in those sentences,
And taking their breakfast in the letter home.
We sat down on the clean grass, in the Garden;
Around us strawberries, cherries, gooseberries, currants
Were ripening, though not yet ready for use ...

An unluxurious incense, intense, dry, pure,
Rises from this letter and from his life.
The morning air seemed to take up the song of our praise.
It is a wonderful honor to be here and to do good.
The river is flowing past the hospital,
Nearly as wide as the Delaware at Trenton,
And, like it, shallow. I can see the young men walking
Through the early streets, on the way to the hospital,
With paper, jellies, and clothing, all laden down.
The morning vapor is rising from the river.
There were about 200, some of them so young.
We wrote letters for them, bound up wounds, prepared
Delicacies. We prayed, and sang "A Charge to Keep."
The incense has the odor of old paper.

Photographs from a Book

i

A poem again, of several parts, each having to do
With a photograph. The first, by Eakins, is of his student,
Samuel C. Murray, about twenty-five years old,
Naked, a life study, in the cold light and hungry
Shadow of Eakins's studio in Philadelphia.
The picture was taken in eighteen ninety-two.
The young man's face is unsmiling, shy, or appears to be so
Because of the shadow. One knows from other
Images in the book that Murray's unshadowed gaze
Can look out clear, untroubled, without mystery or guile.
His body is easy in its selfhood, in its self and strength;
The virtue of its perfection is only of its moment
In the light and shadow. In the stillness of the photograph
I cannot see the light and shadow moving
As light and shadow move in the moving of a river.

ii

He stands against what looks like the other side
Of a free-standing bookcase, with a black cloth
Draped over it, and a shelf as the top of it,
And on the shelf, sad, some bits and pieces
Of old `fine' culture and bric-a-brac:
An urn; a child's head; a carved animal
Of some sort, a dog or a wolf, it's hard to tell;
A bust of a goddess staring out at nothing;
Something floral made of wood or plaster.
"The Arcadians inhabited the earth
Before the birth of Jupiter; their tribe
Was older than the moon. Not as yet
Enhanced by discipline or manners, their life
Resembled that of beasts; they were an uncouth
People, who were still ignorant of art."

iii

There is a strange, solemn, silent, graceless
Gaiety in their dancing, the dancing of the young
Ladies of Philadelphia in the anxious
Saffron light of Eakins's photograph;
There in the nineteenth century, dressed in their `Grecian'
Long white dresses, so many years ago,
They are dancing or standing still before the camera,
Selfhood altered to an alien poetry,
The flowers in their hair already fading;
Persephone, Dryope, Lotis, or maybe only
Some general Philadelphia notion of Grecian
Nymph or maiden, posing, there by the river.
"If those who suffer are to be believed,
I swear by the gods my fate is undeserved."
The light in Eakins's photograph is ancient.

iv

Plate 134. By Eakins. "A cowboy in the West.
An unidentified man at the Badger Company Ranch."
His hat, his gun, his gloves, his chair, his place
In the sun. He sits with his feet in a dried-up pool
Of sunlight. His face is the face of a hero
Who has read nothing at all about heroes.
He is without splendor, utterly without
The amazement of self that glorifies Achilles
The sunlike, the killer. He is without mercy
As he is without the imagination that he is
Without mercy. There is nothing to the East of him
Except the camera, which is almost entirely without
Understanding of what it sees in him,
His hat, his gun, his gloves, his homely and
Heartbreaking canteen, empty on the ground.

Photographs from a Book

v

The Anasazi drink from underground rivers.
The petroglyph cries out in the silence of the rock
The tourist looks at. The past is beautiful.
How few the implements and how carefully made
The dwelling place, against the wind and heat.
Looking at a photograph, as at a petroglyph,
How little there is to go on. "The darkest objects
Reflect almost no light, or none at all,
Causing no changes in the salt in the emulsion."
In the brilliant light and heart-stifling heat,
The scratchings on the surface of the rock,
Utterings, scriptions, bafflings of the spirit,
The bewildered eye reads nonsense in the dazzle;
In the black depth of the rock the river says nothing,
Reflectionless, swift, intent, purposeless, flowing.

vi

A picture of Eakins and a couple of other people,
One of them Murray, bathing in a river,
The Cohansey, near Fairton, New Jersey; Eakins
An old man, Murray not young; the other man,
Elderly, smiling, "probably Charlie Boyers."
They are patiently waiting for the picture to be taken.
It is a summer evening. The photograph
Is overexposed, so the light and the water are almost
Impossible to distinguish one from the other,
In their mutual weakness; an oarless rowboat waits
In the water, just clear of the rivergrass and weeds;
The opposite bank of the river is hard to see
In the washy blankness of the light; the sallow
Flat South Jersey landscape, treeless almost,
Almost featureless, stretches vaguely beyond.

Counterpart

A counterpart to the one my great-grandfather
Wrote lines of, in his letter home: the ripening
Fruit, the purity of intention and deed
In the context of blood and error, the river
That has flowed in every man's ear from generation
To generation. When my great-grandfather preached,
One day, "a wonderful visitation of
The Holy Spirit came down upon the church.
It seemed to fall on men and women alike
Until upon all there was one baptism of the Holy
Fire, and he was thus in his little church
Consecrated to God in the work of preaching."

I found the letter in a metal box in my dead father's
Apartment; the place was shadowy even in the daytime;
Mild, early in September, quiet outside
On the street, and in the apartment; the television
Going, the sound turned off, images flickering
And fluttering inside the lighted screen,
Shaking and gesturing, beseeching the attention.
The ink of the faded ancient writing flowed
Across the page, flowed and lapsed, lapsed into
Forgetfulness; the morning air, the blankness
Of the light, a vapor, a shadow moving,
An unidentified man, selfhood altered.
"I am a child of the earth and of the sky.
But give me quickly the cold water to drink
That flows from Memory's source, from Lebadeia."

Graveyard

A writing I can't read myself: the picture
Of my father, taken a couple of years
Before he died; he is sitting alone some place
I don't know; maybe one of the meetings
He took to going to, trying to keep
His place in the world; he is smiling a little,
Cigarette smoke drifting away; he looks
Courteous, as always, not easy to know.

The side of a hill, nothing but a place;
Grass, dirt, a few scattered sticks, some stones,
The shadow of a tree; *Eurydice*,
My father; speaking the words as they are spoken
The meaning closes itself up; a manuscript
Written in a language only the dead speak.

At Lake Hopatcong

A picture taken years before I was born:
My mother, her sister Sis Nellie, their mother,
Whose name was Emma Saunders Russell, holding

My sister Penelope, a babe in arms,
My father in a stiff high collar and a boater.
My mother is smiling, her hand on her hip. She's wearing

A large hat (is it a toque?) with a high dark
Upstanding feather. Sis Nellie and my mother
Are standing sideways to the car, their faces

Turned to the camera, so that together they frame
The ikon of my grandmother and my sister.
I recognize from later memories

Sis Nellie's stylish intelligent-looking face,
The elegant round gold glasses. She is wearing
A tweed coat of some relatively light color,

And a hat with a narrow brim but full above,
Gathered by a silver buckle to a peak.
My mother's wearing a dark coat with an open collar,

Showing the white blouse over a dark skirt.
The blouse has dark buttons. The family group
Is standing in front of a high auto with tall

Thin wheels, with narrow tires and wooden spokes,
And a canvas top, a beautiful grill adorned
By a radiator cap that looks like a saltcellar.

There is a fluent decoration painted
As if incised on the surface of the hood,
Of the kind that you still can see, painted on trucks,

At Lake Hopatcong

That gives them their incongruous feminine charm
And delicacy, as if the figuration
Was music playing across the metal surface.

The canvas roof of the car's like a little tent
Or pavilion someone put up to celebrate
Their Sunday outing in New Jersey, in nineteen-

Seventeen. Probably the picture is being taken
By Uncle Frank, Sis Nellie's impotent husband.
Maybe because of the limits of the camera

The sky is hard to read. Impossible to tell
The time of year on that weekend afternoon.
I think I can read in her witty-looking face,

From things a doctor told us many years later,
Some things about Nellie's subsequent life which she
Was already concealing and concealed her whole life long,

Her lifelong unbroken hymen, and I therefore know
Some things she didn't know about yet, or was only
Part way through knowing about, in all the story

Of that future, the frustrated sexuality turned
Into malice abetted and invigorated
By the cultural verve and ignorance of the place

And circumstance in which she was brought up,
At Willoughby Spit, near Ocean View, at Norfolk.
But in my grandmother's face there's little to read,

Because I know little about her, so I take her
Almost "as she is," a pleasantfaced woman,
Obviously with trouble with her teeth,

At Lake Hopatcong

As seen by the conformation of her mouth,
Smiling without opening her lips. All I know of her
Is that my mother said she was sweetnatured

And full of equanimity; my sister's
Memories of her in my sister's early childhood
Seem to confirm this. And I know that my grandmother,

As a young girl, was given away to others,
From one family with many children
To another, cousins, or friends, kissing kin,

With none. Saunders is I guess the family name
She was given into. My father looks `handsome and youthful.'
His shoes are brightly shining, and he's wearing

A dark vest and a vestchain under his coat.
I'm puzzled about the straw hat that he's wearing,
Since the womens' coats (my grandmother's also wearing

A heavylooking coat, black, like her hat,
Because she was widowed just a few years before)
Look heavy, wintry, or at least autumnal.

The trees look thinly leaved, as if it were
Late autumn, early spring, or winter in a place
Where dead leaves cling to trees all winter long.

You cannot tell what weather or season it is.
My mother, as in all these early pictures,
Although in this one already having lost

Her girlish slimness, looks sexually alive,
Full of energy, her hair dark, abundant,
Her smile generous (though maybe less so than

In the pictures taken a few years earlier).
Somewhere in this picture there is inscribed
The source or secret, somewhere inscribed the cause,

Of the anxious motherly torment of disapproval,
The torment not resisted by my father,
Visited by my mother on my sister,

The baby in the picture, torment that was
Perhaps in turn the cause of the alcoholism
That, many years later, the baby in the picture

Won out over. But it's all unreadable
In this charming family photograph which, somehow,
Perhaps because of the blankness of the sky,

Looks Russian, foreign, of no country I know.

My Mother's Dying

I listen at the door.
Who's dying, then?
It's like bird-watching.

Who's going to die next?
Birds in the nest.
Who knows about all this?

Willoughby Spit

The little fence around the tiny front yard
Seemed very little even to a child.

Even as a child, visiting there from the North
For a week or maybe two weeks every summer,

I experienced the place as if I had been reading
In a book that was written for very young children to read,

Vivid, crude, charming, frightening in the way
It simplified some truth about the world

You didn't know enough to know about.
There were a few flowers in the little front yard,

Ineptly shaped by nature, looking as if
Someone in a hurry had stuck them in the sand.

There were some boards for getting across the sand
From the gate to the front porch steps. The boards were burning

Under your feet with an intensity
That took your breath away. It was so hot

You could smell the heat of the old gray boards
Of the little walk and the fence as if they might

Burst into smokeless flame at any moment.
The sand of the beach across the street was dark.

It was a surprise to step on it and find
That it was burning dry, although in fact

The flat dull waters of the bay had been
Known to rise up in rage and smite the shore

And get all the way to the road that divided the Spit
And even across it, and even across the sand

On the other side of the road, almost to reach
The smaller bay beyond. The other houses

Were mostly those of strangers, though of course
Not all of them were strangers to Aunt Nellie.

But hardly any were friends since she was bound
Within the spell her eccentricity drew

Like a magic circle around her in the sand,
So none might enter. In the sands behind the houses

There were scrub pines, and living in the woodshed
Behind Aunt Nellie's house were black widow spiders,

So I was told. In the little dark parlor of the house
There was an upright piano, table lamps

With lampshades with beads along their lower edges;
There was a rocker, made of some very dark wood,

Varnished almost black; a couple of other armchairs,
Highbacked, perhaps of the same wood but

With needlepoint-covered seats, and one of them
With needlepoint oval insets on the arms;

On a table, a newspaper, called (I think) the Pilot,
Telling, perhaps, the story of how a drunken

Sailor on the roller coaster that used
To tower high above the other attractions

At Ocean View Amusement Park nearby
Like the skeleton of a dinosaur

Had stood up just as the car tipped over the highest
Point of the highest loop and how he fell

Straight down to his death while the car plunged down
On its thrilling tracks, entirely unconcerned.

Or else it was from a Ferris wheel that he fell,
Just as the wheel had brought him to the top,

And when he stood up the footboard under his feet
Seemed to rock back and forward and back and forward,

Then poured him out over and down, a little figure
Vividly clear as he fell in the story I heard

Of a roller coaster or Ferris wheel back then.
How long ago the sailor must have forgotten

The manner of his death. On the piano were
Some pages of sheet music. "In the gloaming,

Oh my darling, when the lights are burning low,
And the shadows of the evening softly come

And softly go." In the summer heat the door in
From the front porch was always a little bit open

But the light from outside got only a little way in.
On another table a candy dish or ashtray

Decorated with a woman's head, with marcelled
Golden hair and a Grecian profile, expressing

Willoughby Split

Some noble outrage or otherwise disturbed
Emotion, for example, catastrophic loss.

There was a curtain, beaded also, I think,
Between the living room and the dining room

That loomed in littleness beyond. There was a huge
Dining room table and a huge `sideboard,'

The two of them so big you'd have thought the room
Had to be built around them to get them in,

Inherited long ago from a larger house,
Or a wedding present with larger expectations.

And next to this was the dark bedroom in which
Aunt Nellie and her husband, Uncle Frank,

Slept together in sexless affection, as if
In secret collusion. On the bedroom dresser

There was a hairnet, a box containing pins,
Straight pins and safety, mixed in with jewelry –

Brooches, and earrings, bracelets, and other such things.
They glinted in the darkness of the room.

In the sand out back of the house there were those little
Black (or dark purple) pods or podlike things,

Some kind of seaweed which on the beach up North,
In New Jersey, I liked to pick up and burst

Between my fingers. But here, because of the spiders,
They reminded me of them and I didn't touch them.

Aunt Nellie's picture was in the paper once,
Triumphantly posing with a large bottle,

Black widow spiders inside looking out,
As conscious as fireflies of their situation.

At the Hospital

As with the soft authority of wings
Obscurely rustling, angels, we, or else
Expressionless as policemen, in our clothes,
Carefully unaccusing brought the word
Of our health and gladness as we passed along
The shining hospital corridor in the brilliant
Frightening Sixties to the final place
Where on her wretched bed my sister Betts
Lay dying at the bottom of her room.

Above her head, on the television screen,
Endlessly dying on the hotel floor
Lay Bobby Kennedy as about him danced
The dance of consternation flittering out
Along the echoing channels of the night.

To Sally

Now we've been sitting up all night,
    Waiting to find out
        What the story is.

I watch your beautiful patient face:
    It's as if you didn't know
        All that you know.

Your mother in mortal danger, you speak
    Of something funny that happened.
        What will have happened,

Maybe, before your story's finished?
    Good people are punished
        Like all the rest.

A Tomb at Tarquinia

The two of us, on the livingroom couch,
An Etruscan couple,
Blindeyed to the new light let suddenly in;
Sitting among the things that belong to us,
The style of living familiar and easy,
Nothing yet utterly lost.

Leapers and dolphins adorn the painted walls;
The sun is rising,
Or setting, over a blue Tyrrhenian Sea;
In the pictured cup the wine brims and glistens;
An unknown flower burns with odorless incense
The still air of the place.

VI

Mary in Old Age

Yet, though dread Powers, that work in mystery, spin
Entanglings of the brain; though shadows stretch
O'er the chilled heart – reflect, far, far within,
Hers is a holy Being, freed from Sin,
She is not what she seems, a forlorn Wretch,
But delegated Spirits comforts fetch
To her from heights that reason may not win.

– Wordsworth

i

Mary's House

The bruised eyes and diffused radiant
Face, anger *and* joy fused
In a question,
By what possible measure contained?

A skull's blood beating entirely
Uninstructed against
Whatever the world withheld against
The answer.

Nobody knew the answer.
The trees' dark bodies pressed up
Against the house, like night by day,
How like a night by night.

ii

Mary's Room at the Nursing Home

The room was like a room in a rented house
By the sea in the summer. The sun shone in

Mary in Old Age

Flatly and plainly, and sunlight and shadow
Were disposed forthrightly and reasonably

Across the surface of things, for instance on
The brown linoleum floor or on the simple

Pine table painted a chalky green. There were decal
Flowers on the headboard and footboard of the bed,

Ignorant and cheerful about where they were.
As in a room to which one goes on vacation,

A rented place by the sea, there were very few
Things one could call one's own, and these had a vivid

Prominence: an open book on a table,
A vase of blue and white cornflowers, a brass clock.

Can Mary have been reading? Is the madness a hoax?
But the book on the table was a Harlequin romance

The attendant must just that moment have left off reading.
It was hot as anything. The curtains mimed

The letting in of air. Strangely girlish and wasted,
Mary lay on the little single bed

In a flowered summer dress, a naked Maja,
Or like Olympia in the painting by Manet,

Careless of everything, wanton, royal.

iii

The Tower of Babel

She babbled barbarously and bravely,
With bravado and bravura,
A baby in a babushka, with a balalaika.
She was "a gate of God," a Babeler,
"Though babbling only to the Vale
Of sunshine and of flowers,
Bringing unto me a tale
Of visionary hours."

iv

Of Others Who Were There

There was: the old lady in the nursing home
Who kept coming up to me and standing much too close
To me, sniffing at my body or my soul
As if it was something deliciously stinking,

Thrilling to her, or else a flowering bush,
Nourishment for a ravenous questioning;
Staring into my ear the way the child
In the comic routine long ago in the movies

Stared silently into the coils of the ear
Of the man sitting there next to the child,
Trying to watch the movie on the screen,
Driven wild inside by the child's relentless gaze:

As if the ear could speak its secrets back

v

Mary Interpreter

Not a babble exactly, but words carefully chosen
To question the nature of her experience

In the bafflement of its own imprisoning nonsense.
Of the flowers I brought her on that summer day:

"When are you going to take them home and use them?"
And, "Yes, they were here, but I didn't see them,"

And, looking once again at the bouquet,
More closely, earnestly, and with suspicion:

"What is that? *Why did it go wrong?*"
Rocking a little in the rocking chair, she said,

"*I don't want to stay here. I want to stop it.*"
Was "here" the nursing home? Was it the chair?

The condition she was in? Her life? Life? The body?
Which of these things was it she wanted to stop?

Was she imprisoned in a world whose meanings
She was so familiar with that she needed to make

No translations at all, and no translation would be
Anything but fatuous? Thus "Life" seems melodramatic,

Too large and general to fit the case.
But "the chair" seems too small. And "the nursing home"

Too obviously the right answer to be so.
In my reason and health I was outside this world,

Translating her words with a too easy confidence.
But Mary was there, imprisoned in it, sovereign.

The scene changed in the way I experienced it.
It was as if I wasn't in the room

But in the empty lobby of some building.
Mary was in an open elevator,

Old-fashioned, ornate, and beautiful.
The elevator kept moving up and down,

Kept going down to the hell below – when I
Leaned over and looked down then I could see

The suffering and also I could hear
Sounds of the suffering too – then up again

To the hellish heaven above – peering up there
Through the elevator shaft I saw and heard

The transcendental hilarious suffering there.
I heard voices as if there was singing or quarreling.

The Otis elevator never stopped at all.
Mary's body and spirit kept passing back and forth

Before my eyes, vivid, free of the conditions
In terms of which her sympathetic friend,

Standing in the deserted hallway, saw her
Carried up and down in the elevator.

Over and over I saw her going past,
Clinging to the bars, gesticulating,

Frantic, confusingly like a figure of joy.
In the heat of the room on the summer day

Mary, standing now, began to unzip her dress,
With a slowness and persistence that suggested

An indecent purpose, a naked revelation
Of body or soul, embarrassing to a visitor

There at the nursing home on a kind errand.
Perhaps she only wanted to unzip the dress

A little way, because of the summer heat.
But something about it seemed to refuse the suggestion.

There was a concentration and seriousness,
Oblivious of the visitor and his thoughts,

As when she looked so earnestly at the bouquet.
We were in the same room and not in the same room.

I was in the same room. She was in a shirt of fire.
She was out on a plain crossed by steppewinds.

vi

Matthew 12: 43-45

When the unclean spirit goes out of a person,
She walks for days and nights through the dry places,
Looking for rest, and never finding any.
And then she says, "I will go home to my house,

From which I came." And so Mary goes there.
She finds it nicely swept and cleanly kept,
And pleasantly furnished, and garnished with flowers,
And empty, as if waiting for her to come home.

And then the unclean spirit goes and finds the other
Unclean spirits. They come to her house together,
And get into the house, and live there, and it is worse
For her, much worse, than it had earlier been.

Character Analysis of Mary in Earlier Life

Her spinster eccentricity often
Said things for the sake of startling you.

She was like that. It seemed a form of shyness,
Putting you off with her charm flirtatiously.

It was a powerful entrapped wild innocent conventional nature.

The rage in her charm steadily
Burned its way through the materials of her life

So that there was always almost nothing left.
To put it another way:

Where she was was always on a high platform
She got to on high heels getting across

On a tightrope strung out over the abyss.

Multas Per Gentes

– Catullus CI

O my poor brother, I have journeyed here,
  Through many foreign lands and many seas,
To come to this unhappy ceremony,
  Seeking to speak to ashes that cannot speak,
Since Fortune has taken you yourself from me –
  Alas, my brother, cruelly taken you.

According to the custom of our fathers,
  I bring these offerings for the wretched dead.
Accept, my brother, what I have brought you, weeping.
  Ave, forever *vale*, my poor brother.

Martial i. 101

He, who had been the one to whom I had
Recited my poems and then he wrote them down
With his faithful scribal hand for which already
He was well known and had been justly praised,
Demetrius has died. He lived to be
Fifteen years old, and after that four summers.
Even the Caesars had heard how good he was.

When he fell sick and I knew he was going to die,
I didn't want him to descend to where
The Stygian shades are, still a slave, and so
I relinquished my ownership of him to his sickness.
Deserving by my deed to have gotten well,
He knew what I had done and was grateful for it,
Calling me his patron, falling free,

Down to those waters that are waiting there.

That Evening at Dinner

By the last few times we saw her it was clear
That things were different. When you tried to help her
Get out of the car or get from the car to the door
Or across the apartment house hall to the elevator
There was a new sense of heaviness
Or of inertia in the body. It wasn't
That she was less willing to be helped to walk
But that the walking itself had become less willing.
Maybe the stupid demogorgon blind
Recalcitrance of body, resentful of the laws
Of mind and spirit, was getting its own back now,
Or maybe a new and subtle alien
Intelligence of body was obedient now
To other laws: "Weight is the measure of
The force with which a body is drawn downward
To the center of the earth"; "Inertia is
The tendency of a body to resist
Proceeding to its fate in any way
Other than that determined for itself."

That evening, at the Bromells' apartment, after
She had been carried up through the rational structure
By articulate stages, floor after flashing floor,
And after we helped her get across the hall,
And get across the room to a chair, somehow
We got her seated in a chair that was placed
A little too far away from the nearest table,
At the edge of the abyss, and there she sat,
Exposed, her body the object of our attention –
The heaviness of it, the helpless graceless leg,
The thick stocking, the leg brace, the medical shoe.

At work between herself and us there was
A new principle of social awkwardness
And skillfulness required of each of us.
Our tones of voice in this easy conversation

Were instruments of marvelous finesse,
Measuring and maintaining with exactitude
"The fact or condition of the difference
There was between us, both in space and time."
Her smiling made her look as if she had
Just then tasted something delicious, the charm
Her courtesy attributed to her friends.

This decent elegant fellow human being
Was seated in virtue, character, disability,
Behind her the order of the ranged bookshelves,
The windows monitored by Venetian blinds –
"These can be raised or lowered; numerous slats,
Horizontally arranged, and parallel,
Which can be tilted so as to admit
Precisely the desired light or air."

We were all her friends, Maggie, and Bill, and Anne,
And I, and the nice Boston Brahmin elderly man
Named Duncan, utterly friendly and benign.
And of course it wasn't whether or not the world
Was benign but whether it looked at her too much.
She wasn't `painfully shy' but just the same
I wouldn't be surprised if there had been
Painfulness in her shyness earlier on,
Say at dancing school. Like others, though, she had
Survived her childhood somehow. Nor do I mean
She was unhappy. Maybe more or less so
Before her marriage. One had the sense of trips
Arranged, committees, concerts, baffled courage
Living it through, giving it order and style.
And one had the sense of the late marriage as of
Two bafflements inventing the sense they made
Together. The marriage seemed, to the outside world,
And probably was, radiant and triumphant,
And I think that one could almost certainly say

That during the last, heroic, phase of things,
After his death, and after the stroke, she had
By force of character and careful management,
Maintained a certain degree of happiness.

The books there on the bookshelves told their stories,
Line after line, all of them evenly spaced,
And spaces between the words. You could fall through the spaces.
In one of the books Dr. Johnson told the story:
"In the scale of being, wherever it begins,
Or ends, there are chasms infinitely deep;
Infinite vacuities. For surely,
Nothing can so disturb the passion, or
Perplex the intellects of man so much,
As the disruption of this union with
Visible nature, separation from all
That has delighted or engaged him, a change
Not only of the place but of the manner
Of his being, an entrance into a state
Not simply which he knows not, but perhaps
A state he has not faculties to know."

The dinner was delicious, fresh greens, and reds,
And yellows, produce of the season due,
And fish from the nearby sea; and there were also
Ashes to be eaten, and dirt to drink.

The Death of Enkidu

– from Gilgamesh, *Tablet Seven*

In the early hours of the next morning dawning,
Enkidu lay in his bed, fear in his belly.

He told a dream to Gilgamesh who was there.
"I had a dream. There was a noise in the sky

and a noise in the earth in answer. On a dark plain
I was alone. But there was one, a man,

with a lion head, and the paws of a lion too,
but the nails were talons, the talons of an eagle.

The face was dark. He took hold of me and seized me.
I fought with him, I hit at him, but he

kept moving about in the dark, too quick for me,
and then with a blow he capsized me like a raft.

I cried out in the dark to Gilgamesh,
'Two people, companions,' but the man overpowered me,

and raged like a wild bull over me in glory,
and Gilgamesh was afraid and did not help me.

Then I was changed into something like a bird,
with a bird's arms, as spindly as a bird's,

and feathered like a bird. He seized an arm
and led me to the dwelling of Irkalla,

the House of Darkness, the House of No Return.
No one comes back who ever enters there.

The garments that they wear are made of feathers.
The food they eat is clay, the drink is dirt.

The Death of Enkidu

Stillness and dust are on the door and door bolt.
There is no light of any sort at all.

Dead kings were there, and princes of old kingdoms,
dead high priests and acolytes were there,

dead chanters and anointers, bearers of ointments;
Etana was there and Sumuqan was there,

and on her throne Ereshkigal the Queen
of the Underworld, and kneeling before her was

Belit-Seri the Scribe who holds the tablet
on which the fate of everyone is written.

She turned her head and looked at us and said:
'Who has led here this latest to arrive?'"

Gilgamesh said: "The dream is terrible."
Enkidu said: "We went together through

the dangers of the Forest and we killed
the Bull of Heaven. Do not forget how we,

two people together, prevailed against the terror."
Enkidu lay suffering on the bed of terror

another day and another day and another,
and the long nights between, and day after day

the suffering of Enkidu grew worse.
On the twelfth day he raised up in his bed

and spoke these words to Gilgamesh and said:
"Gilgamesh, who encouraged me in the battle,

saying, 'Two people, companions, they can prevail,'
Gilgamesh is afraid and does not help me!"

After that Gilgamesh heard the death rattle.

Brunswick, Maine, Early Winter, 2000

That day when Suzie drove us out to get
The lobsters at the lobster place at the cove:

Bill Moran in the passenger seat of the car,
Doubled up as if in a fit of laughter,

A paroxysm of helpless, silent laughter,
At the joke the Parkinson's had played on him.

The big joke he simply couldn't get over.

*

Bill Moran at breakfast time, in the kitchen,
Bent double in his wheel chair, his chin almost

Touching the kitchen table, and his eyes
Intently studying a piece of toast,

A just discovered, as yet unreadable
Mesopotamian language, not related

To Akkadian or Sumerian, much older
Even than what he knew about already –

The great old man with his ferocity
Of tenderness and joy, his eyes intently

Studying the text. He sent me once
A passage copied from Nietzsche's book *Daybreak*:

"It is a connoisseurship of the word;
Philology is that venerable art

That asks one thing above all other things:
Read slowly, slowly. It is a goldsmith's art,

Looking before and after, cautiously;
Considering; reconsidering;

Studying with delicate eyes and fingers.
It does not easily get anything done."

Bill looking for heaven on the tabletop.

*

After the funeral Suzie said, "Bill thought
He'd be flying around up there somewhere forever."

And he could fly. After breakfast that day
We wheeled him away from the kitchen table and into

The living room and there was a frame contraption
Set up on long thin cranelike legs. It looked

Like something in a children's playground, with
A canvas sling to carry him through the air

From the wheel chair to another chair; heartbreaking,
Swaddled, small, ridiculously like

A newborn baby. Or else the sling resembled
Those slings you see on television when

They rescue people from their sinking boats
And carry them up under the angel wings

To safety in the helicopter noise.

VII

Shubshi-meshre-Shakkan

– Babylonian

Hymn

I sing this hymn in praise of him who is
The wisest of all, raging in darkness, or,
In the bright morning, calm, the wisest of all.

The storm of his anger it is that lays the land low;
His breath in the quiet morning stirs but a leaf;
The flood of his anger cannot be withstood.

He is the lord who pities and forgives.
The sky will buckle under the weight of his hands;
He holds the sick man gently in his hands.

The thorns of his whip cut into the flesh and it bleeds;
His poultice cools and eases the body's pain;
It eases the pain and the wounded body heals.

He has but to frown and the strength departs from a man;
The strength departs from a man and the man is weak.
The Lady Fortune departs, seeking out others.

He smiles and the personal god comes back to the man,
His strength comes back to the man and re-enters his body.
The Lady Fortune returns from where she had gone to.

Narrative

i

Everywhere around me there is confusion.
Enlil and the other gods have given me up.

Shubshi-meshre-Shakkan

The personal god has gone away from my house.
The Lady Fortune has gone to somebody else.

I see the omens everywhere I look.
The king, the sun that shines on his happy people,

The king is angry and he will not hear me.
When I go to the palace now, they look at me.

One person blinks and another looks away.
What are these omens? How is it I should read them?

When I lie down to dream I have nightmares.
In the street I see the others looking at me.

I see how people point their fingers at me.
I hear them talking about me in the street.

One says: "I made him want to end his life,"
One says: "I will take over his position,

I'll be the one who goes and lives in his house ..."
Six or seven talking in the street,

Six or seven gathered in the street,
Storm demons raging against me in the street.

*

The year has turned and everywhere I see
Wherever I look the signs of my bad luck.

I cannot find out anywhere what is right.
I pray to my personal god and he doesn't answer.

I pray to the Lady Fortune, she will not listen.
I went to the dream interpreter, he poured

Libations to the gods but they said nothing.
The zaqiqu spirit said nothing; nothing was what

Could be done by the one whose charms can charm away
The evil spirits. Everywhere around me

There is confusion. Everything is strange.

*

It is as if I did not pray to the gods.
It is as if I did not properly say

The name of the goddess before I eat my meal.
It is as if I did not teach my household

How to honor the gods. It is as if
I taught my household people how to neglect

The holy days and festivals of the year.
I kept the rules; to worship was my joy;

The music of the procession delighted me;
Before I ate I spoke the name of my god;

I taught my people how to honor the gods,
And to honor the king as if he were a god.

I taught my people how to respect the palace.
I wish I knew these things would please the gods.

Shubshi-meshre-Shakkan

I wish I knew the meaning of these things.
Who knows the will of the gods in heaven? Who knows?

Maybe the gods despise what men think right.
Maybe what men think wrong delights the gods.

Who knows the ways of the gods of the Underworld?
What man has ever learned the ways of the gods?

Today he is dead who was living yesterday;
From gladness to sorrow is but the blink of an eye;

He sings in joy this moment who wails the next.

ii

Around me everywhere there is confusion.
Everything is strange. A storm wind drives me along.

Sickness has come upon me. An evil wind
Has blown in from the horizon. As new little plants

Come up through the ground in spring when their time has come,
The Weakness comes up through the ground. The Coughing
                                                        comes up,

It comes up horribly laughing out of the abyss.
The Headache comes up out of the Underworld.

The Bone-Ache comes from the surface of the waters.
The Lamashtu-demon comes down from the mountain.

All of the demons gather themselves upon me.
The phlegm fills up my throat and my throat chokes.

Whatever I eat is vile. Beer, solace of men,
Is vile in my mouth. Grain is vile in my mouth.

All night the demons torment me, What are they saying?
I cannot hear what it is that they are saying.

Where has my dignity gone, and my good looks?
The exorcist has nothing to say. The diviner

Has nothing to say. My personal god has not
Come to my rescue. The Lady Fortune has not.

My chest was broad, my arms were strong, and now
A boy could easily wrestle me to the ground.

My looks are strange. The flesh is loose on my bones.
I try to walk. My feet have forgotten how.

My knees are fettered and bound like the busu-bird's.
At night I lie in my shit like an ox or a sheep.

My grave is open already and waiting. Already
All the funeral things have been prepared.

He who gloats gloats when he hears about it.
She who gloats gloats when she hears about it.

The day is dark for all my family.
For all my friends lamenting the day is dark.

iii

His hand was heavy upon me, I could not bear
The weight of his hand, I could not bear the fear

Of the storm wind screaming against me and blowing against me.
I lay awake or else I was asleep.

There was a young man, beautiful, wearing new garments.
I dreamed a priest was holding in his hand

A bough of tamarisk that purifies.
There was a young woman came to me in my dream.

Beautiful, wearing new garments. She spoke to me:
"Here is deliverance from your wretchedness."

There was a young man came to me in my dream,
Bearded, wearing a headdress. He carried a tablet

And on the tablet written was a message:
"Marduk has sent me. I come to bring you luck.

To Shubshi-meshre-Shakkan I bring good luck."
The storm of Marduk's anger was quieted down.

A lion was eating me. Marduk muzzled the lion.
Marduk took my hand and raised me up.

He who had thrown me down he raised me up.
My knees, which were fettered and bound like the busu-bird's,

My knees were freed from their bonds and I could walk.

My throat, which was closed, was opened, and I sang.

Hymn

The Babylonians saw what Marduk had done
And everything they said proclaimed his greatness,
The storm of his anger it is that lays the land low;

His breath in the quiet morning stirs but a leaf;
The flood of his anger cannot be withstood.
He is the lord who pities and forgives.

Who would have thought this man would see the sun?
Who would have thought this man would walk again?
Who would have thought we would see him on the street?

What god but Marduk could bring back the dying?
Who would have thought this man would see the sun?
Who would have thought we would see him on the street?

As far as the land extends and the sky above it,
Wherever the sun god shines and the fire burns,
Wherever the waters are and where the winds blow,

Wherever the creatures are whom the goddess Aruru
Fashioned of clay, endowed with breath and life,
The black-headed creatures, men, who walk the earth,

Let there be praise for Marduk for what he has done.

The Offering of Isaac

– from Genesis A, Anglo-Saxon

Then the Lord wanted to know
    How steadfast was his man,
So He said, in the Lord's stern voice,
    "Abraham, Abraham, you
Must take your belovèd child,
    Your own, your only son,
And go with him to where
    I will show you what to do.
A place there is, high in the hills.
    You must climb up there on foot.
The two of you together,
    Around you only nothing,
Only the mountain peaks
    Around you witnessing.
And there make ready a fire,
    A bale-fire for your bairn,
And then, you must, yourself,
    Take up the sword you carry,
And kill him with its edge,
    And burn his dear body black
In the flames you have set going
    And present what you have done,
A burnt offering to Me."

        Abraham heard the Lord
And did not put off the journey.
    At once he made his way,
Determined and intent
    On the task that he had been
Commanded to undertake.
    He was in awe of the Word
Of the Lord God of angels.
    He was the Lord's servant,
Eager to please his Master.
    Blessèd was Abraham.

Without any night-rest
    He got up from his bed.
He obeyed without any question
    The commandment of the Lord.
He girded on his sword,
    Fear of the Lord's Word
Continual in his breast.
    That good old man, the giver
Of rings to his followers,
    He harnessed and bridled his asses,
And selected from his household
    Two young men, and told them
To go with him on his journey.
    Isaac his half-grown son
Was the third one of the party.
    He was himself the fourth.
So together they went to do
    The bidding of the Lord,
Hastening on their way
    Across the deserted landscape,
Until, on the third day,
    The bright light of the morning
Rose up from the deep water,
    Where everything begins.

There, then, the blessèd man
    Looked up and saw the high
Mountain that the Lord
    Had told him they were to go to.
Abraham spoke to the two
    Retainers and said, "My men,
Stay here where we have camped.
    We will return when we
Have carried out what the King
    Of souls has told us to do."
Then Abraham left them and went

The Offering of Isaac

Up onto the high mountain,
Climbing through woods and groves,
    Taking his own son with him.
The son carried the wood,
    The father carried the fire,
And was carrying the sword.
    Then his belovèd son,
Trudging beside his father,
    Said to his father, "Father,
We're carrying the wood,
    The fire, and the sword,
To do what the bright Lord
    Asks us to do, but where
Is the sacrificial victim?
    Where is the offering
To put upon the fire"?
    His father, who was steadfast,
Faithful to what the Creator
    Had told him to do, replied
"He, who is the true
    King, the Guardian,
Protector of His people,
    He will find what is right
And what is fitting for this."
    Then, obedient, resolute,
Steadfast, he went on climbing
    Up the steep mountain with
His only son beside him,
    Until they came to the top,
To the place to which the Lord
    Had told him where to go,
And there he took the sticks
    Of wood his son had carried
And with them made ready the fire,
    Only the mountains around,
Witnessing what he was doing.

Hand and foot he bound
  His own, his only son,
    Young half-grown Isaac,
And lifted his own child up
    And laid him on the pyre,
And took up the sword in his hand
    And stood there ready to kill him,
And for the thirsty fire
    To drink the blood of his boy.

Then suddenly from above
    An angel of the Lord
Called out to Abraham
    In a loud voice, "Abraham!"
Abraham stood still,
    He stood stock-still and listened
And heard the words of the angel.
    "Abraham, do not kill
Your own, your only son.
    Take him up, lift him away
From the pyre you have put him upon.
    The Lord has granted him
Great honor, and you, great scion,
    And patriarch of the Hebrews,
Will be given many rewards
    By the Guardian of Souls,
Because you were willing to
    Sacrifice your son,
Your belovèd only son,
    In obedience to the Lord
And for the love of Him."
    The fire went on burning.

The Creator of Mankind
    Had so approved the heart
Of Abraham, Lot's kinsman,

That God gave him back his bairn
In safety, and alive.
  Then Abraham, the brother
Of Haran, turned his head,
  And looked back over his shoulder,
And saw, not far away,
  A ram caught in the brambles.
Then he took hold of the ram
  And quickly lifted it up
Onto the burning pyre
  And took his sword and killed it,
In place of his own son,
  There on the smoking altar
Stained with the blood of the ram.
  He offered to the Lord
The burnt offering,
  In gratitude for the gifts
He had given them and would give
  Forever and ever after.

VIII

Civilization and Its Discontents

Under the burin's meditative gaze,
Caught in the cross-hatching and close-working
Of the great engraving of the great painting
Fête Vénitienne, entangled in
The entrapment of the scription, as if in vines
Entangled, or the entanglement of the veins,
It is Watteau himself, a naked soul,
Suffering the humiliation and pain
Of the company of fellow human beings,
Dressed up as a country shepherd pretending to play
The bagpipe or musette for them to dance to,
Looking over at what's-his-name, at Vleughels,
Monstrously civilized great Turkey cock
Here shown displaying all his gorgeous plumage
In grandiose dance, while all about in studied
Mutual disposition others were,
And Venus was, presiding over the scene,
And over all this the great embroidered trees.

In Despair

– Cavafy, "En Apognosei"

He's gone from him forever, and ever since he's sought
his lips on the lips of every boy he goes to bed with,
wanting to fool himself into thinking those are the very
lips of the boy he gave himself to, long ago.
But he's gone from him forever, he's never coming back.

He's gone from him forever as if he never was,
because, he said, he wanted to save himself from the shameful
pleasure, unnatural pleasure of what they did together,
the shameful pleasure he wanted to save his body from.
There was still time, he said, to save himself, he said.

He's gone from him forever, as if he never was.
He seeks, hallucinating, self-deluding, seeking
on the lips of other boys the lips of him with whom
that shameful pleasure he'd had he'll never have again.

Catullus II

Little sparrow,

my girl friend's pet delight,

dandling you in her lap,

or letting you

peck at her finger,

or getting you

even to bite it,

A little bit sharply,

when she,

who's the light of my love,

still feels

like playing with you,

like that,

and doing so

in the aftermath

of the quieting down

of her earlier ardor,

in order to

relieve what's left of it,

– ah, I wish

I could play

with you,

just like that,

until,

at last,

that would make me

feel

a lot better.

Dido In Despair

– from Virgil, Aeneid, *IV, ii. 450-474*

Then, truly, wretched Dido, overwhelmed
By knowledge of the fate that has come upon her,
Prays for death; she is weary of looking at
The over-arching sky. And to make sure
That what has been begun will be completed
And that she will depart from the light, she saw
As she set out her ritual offerings
Upon the incense-burning altars, how –
The horror! – the holy water darkened and
The wine was changed to an excremental slime.
She said nothing about this, no, not even to
Her sister. Furthermore, within her palace
There was a marble chapel devoted to
Her husband who had died, and which she had
Wonderfully and faithfully maintained,
Adorning it with leaves and snow-white garlands.
At night, when night possessed the world, she heard,
When she was there, noises that sounded like
Her husband's voice, words calling to her; and too,
She heard the gloomy sound of the owl alone
Upon the city roofs, in long-continued
Wailing lamentation; sometimes she heard
The voices of old sayings of the prophets,
Speaking to her in her head their terrible warnings.
And in her sleep savage Aeneas himself
Drives her before him in her madness; or
Always alone along some vacant street
Unendingly unaccompanied she seeks
To find her Tyrians in an empty land –
It's as when Pentheus, demented, sees
The Furies and, seeing double, sees two suns,
And see two Thebes, two cities, or as when
Agamemnon's son Orestes flees from his mother,
Who is brandishing fire and writhing snakes, and there
In the doorway the Dirae crouch, and patiently wait.

She Speaks Across the Years

– Hölderlin, Wenn aus der ferne ...

"If having gone so far from one another
On distant ways, if across all the ways
And all the time you know me still who was
Your partner in those days in all the sorrow,
Then something after all is left of it all.

Where's she who loved you waiting for you now? –
Here in the Civic Garden, just as before,
Here where in memory once again we're meeting,
In the dusk, as before, and after all the sorrow,
Beside the black original river flowing.

There were those moments, I remember there were those moments,
When you, so closed up in yourself, were able,
With me, to be, if, just for a moment, less so.
There was something good about that, for you, for me.
The time went by as if there was no trouble.

I remember how you showed me all those places
That though this was my country I had never
Visited or seen as through your eyes,
The open fields, and also the hidden places
Looking from concealment out over the sea.

Was it in springtime then? Was it in summer?
The nightingales and the other birds were singing
And the fragrance of the trees was all around us;
And the hyacinth, the violets, the tulips,
Green ivy on the housewalls, green the shadows

Of the pathways where we walked together then,
Thinking it all, after all, was possible.
It wasn't that you were different than you were,
Nor I than I, but that we were for awhile
All right together in our separate selves ... "

The Waiting

Someone hammering something somewhere outside;
The sound of the plumbing faithfully dying away
Somewhere in the building; the ocean noises of cars
From blocks beyond, like the quiet breathing of waves;
The mad young woman waits for her faithful lover;
Her innocent curtains tell her the secrets of summer air.

She stands at her window and waits; somewhere outside
Someone is hammering something; the ocean is breathing;
The mailman has come and gone, he spoke her name;
The curtains whisper a little against the sill;
How often he comes to her door, the imposter, her lover;
He speaks in a secret tongue understood by no other.

Of Violets

– Poliziano

O beautiful violets, seeming to give such promise
Of the fulfillment of love, the gift of her
Whom I love, what is the nectar the tender winds
Have scattered over your petals, making them fragrant?
What is the place of your birth? Was it under the care
Of radiant Venus, there in the fields near the spring
Of Acidalia? Was it under the care
Of the god of love in the Idalian grove?

It must be that these are the same flowers
With which the Muses decorate their lyres
To play upon on the flowerbank of Permessus,
That these are the same flowers with which the maidens
Hora, Gratia, Aurora, have adorned themselves
In the hour of the opening day. These must be the same
Flowers that bloom in the violetbeds of the garden
Of the Hesperides, in the silent grove
The held breath of the wind possesses. These
Violets are the springtime offering of Chloris;
The virtuous shades of the dead come back to play
Among the grasses the violets intersperse.

Too happy violets, which that hand plucked
That wrenched me, miserable, from myself –
She held you, violets, to her lips, perhaps;
Perhaps her lips and breath have breathed on you
The breath of her whom I love, the changing colors
Of her breathing, making you blush and pale;
From the breath of her lips your fragrance is breathed upon you;
The sovereignty of her fragrance clings to you.

O most fortunate violets, who are
My life and my delight, the place of keeping,
The haven of my heart's longing, violets,
Whom I touch and kiss in pain in thought of her,

Of Violets

These tears I shed nourish the fires of love
Whose slow burning issues in these tears.
Be with me now forever, violets;
Let neither the heat of summer nor winter's cold
Deprive me of your solace, solace of pain;
Stay with me now, perpetual in beauty,
O violets, O quietness of heart,
For I am in the wretchedness of love,

Creature of sighs and weeping, because of my lady.

Roman Elegy X

– Goethe

Alexander, Caesar, Henry, Frederick the Great –
    There isn't one who wouldn't give me half
Of what he got being great if he could have
    One single night of what we have together.

Poor things, now Orcus has them in his power.
    You who are living, lovers, revel in pleasure
In love's warm bed before your horrified foot
    All of a sudden recoils from Lethe's touch.

"Quand vous serez bien vieille"

– Ronsard

When you are very old, at night, by candlelight,
Sitting up close to the fire, unwinding or winding the thread,
Marveling you will murmur, telling over the songs of the dead,
"Ronsard praised this body before it became this fright."

Not one of your companions, dozing over her spinning,
But, hearing you say these things in her old woman's dream,
Will be startled half-awake to bless your famous name
For the praise it had deserved of my immortal singing.

I will be under the earth, my body nothing at all,
Taking its rest at last, under the dark myrtle;
There you'll be by the fire, a hunched-up old woman

That held off my love for a long look in the mirror.
Listen to what I say, don't wait for tomorrow:
These flowers in their blossom go quickly out of season.

News from Mount Amiata

– Montale, "Notizie dall'Amiata"

By later tonight the fireworks of the storm
Will be a swarming of bees below the horizon.
I'm writing this letter to you at a wooden table
Whose wood the insects and worms have gotten into.
The beams are pockmarked with their ravenous feasting.
A smell of melon mildew rises from the floor,
As from the valley rises the valley smoke,
As it were the smoke of mushrooms, clouding my window.
Here in the rich core of the world, in this room,
In this honeycomb, mealy, fragrant, innermost cell
Of a sphere launched out across the luminous skies,
You who are elsewhere and other dwell in another
Cell and center of things, but, here at this table,
Writing to you, in front of this fire the chestnuts
Lavishly burst themselves open upon the hearth of,
That life is too brief that invokes your absent presence
Against the glowing background as of an ikon.

Outside the windows the rain is falling ...
                                        If you
Were to make your way among the ancient feeble
Soot-blackened buildings time has made that way,
And along the alleys between them, and through the courtyards
Where in the middle there is a wellhead where
The well goes down forever and forever,
If you could follow the heavy flights of night birds
Down the alleys to where, beyond the ravine,
The galaxy glimmers, the matrix of our torment ...
But the only step that echoes along the darkness
Is that of someone by himself who sees
Shadows of doorways falling, shadows collapsing;
The threads between the stars are lost to sight;
The clock in the campanile is stopped at two;
Even the vines that climb the ancient walls
Are shadows that climb in the dark.

                    North Wind, come down,
Unloosen the hands that clutch the sandstone walls;
Scatter the books of hours on the attic floors.
Clear all away, cold wind, and then, let all
Be clearness of sight that has dominion over
The mind that does not know how to despair.
Cold wind, seal up the spores from which the tendrils
Sprout that then climb as shadows the ancient walls.
These alleys are too narrow; the donkey hooves
That clatter in the darkness on the cobbles
Strike sparks the unseen mountain peak above
Replies to with magnesium random signals;
And oh the leaking slowly deliquescing
Walls of the huddled houses in the rain,
Time turning to water, the endless dialogue
With the wretched dead, the ashes, oh, the wind,
The death, the death that lives ...
                    This Christian fuss –
Nothing but words of shadow and of grief –
What can I say through them that speaks to you?
Less than the water draining away down the runnels.
An old abandoned mill wheel, the trunk of a tree,
Markers of the limits of the world ...
A pile of litter shakes and disintegrates ...
At night the porcupines come out, seeking
A trickle of water to pity them ... They join
My waking vigil to your deep dreaming sleep.

L'anguilla

– *Montale*

Anguilla, eel, sea-siren
That making its way from those
Cold Baltic seas to get to ours,
Our estuaries, deltas,
And into our streams, and from
The profound beneath the river, rises up
Against the downstream impetus of flow,
Upstream from branch to branch and into ever
Smaller capillaries, seeking ever
Evermore to enter
Into the heart of rock, inching through mire,
Until, one afternoon, a flash of light,
Ricocheted off a sunstruck chestnut leaf,
Glints upon the surface
Of a stagnant pool
Or in a dry runnel coming down the side
Of the Appenines,
Down to Romagna; eel, sea-siren,
Candleblink, whiplash, arrow of love,
Which only our arid ditches or
The desiccated Pyrenean vacant streambeds can
Show the way back
To the paradise of fecundation;
Green soul, searching for life
Where only desolation and
Absolute driedupness are;
Scintilla, spark, whose declaration is
That all begins when all is burned to charcoal;
Buried-dead-tree-stump;
Brief iris rainbow glint,
Twin to the one that eyelash-framed
Sets you shining intact among the sons of men
Sunk in your mire;
Do you not see that she is your sister?

IX

Strabo Reading Megasthenes

According to Megasthenes' own account
The wild man has no mouth with which to eat,

But only a breathing-orifice to breathe with.
He lives on the odor of fruits, and of flowers blooming,

Or on the smell of faraway roasting meat.

The Guest Ellen at the Supper for Street People

The unclean spirits cry out in the body
Or mind of the guest Ellen in a loud voice,
Torment me not, and in the fury of her unclean
Hands beating the air in some kind of unending torment –
Nobody witnessing could possibly know the event
That cast upon her the spell of this enchantment.

Almost all the guests are under some kind of enchantment:
Of being poor day after day in the same body;
Of being witness still to some obscene event;
Of listening all the time to somebody's voice
Whispering in the ear things divine or unclean,
In the quotidian of unending torment.

One has to keep thinking there was some source of torment,
Something that happened someplace else, unclean.
One has to keep talking in a reasonable voice
About things done, say, by a father's body
To or upon the body of Ellen, in enchantment
Helpless, still by the unforgotten event

Enchanted, still in the old forgotten event
A prisoner of love, filthy Ellen in her torment,
Guest Ellen in the dining hall in her body,
Hands beating the air in her enchantment,
Sitting alone, gabbling in her garbled voice
The narrative of the spirits of the unclean.

She is wholly the possessed one of the unclean.
Maybe the spirits came from the river. The enchantment
Entered her, maybe, in the Northeast Kingdom. The torment,
A thing of the waters, gratuitous event,
Came up out of the waters and entered her body
And lived in her in torment and cried out in her voice.

It speaks itself over and over again in her voice,
Cursing maybe or not a familiar obscene event
Or only the pure event of original enchantment
From the birth of the river waters, the pure unclean
Rising from the source of things, in a figure of torment
Seeking out Ellen, finding its home in her poor body.

Her body witness is, so also is her voice,
Of torment coming from unknown event;
Unclean is the nature and name of the enchantment.

Lazarus

The dogheaded wildman sleeps in the back alley,
Behind the fence with bittersweet adorned,
In the corner of the garden over near
Where the viburnum flowers or fails to flower,
Depending on whether or not we water it.
Many times over again it has survived.
The leaves are homely, crudely rough-cut, with
A texture like sandpaper; an unluscious green,
Virtuous in look, not really attractive;
Like Kent in *Lear* plainspoken, a truth-teller,
Impatient with comparison as with deceit.

The wildman sleeps in the maple-shaded alley
Hidden behind the garden fence behind
The wooden garden seat weathering gray
In the corner of the garden over near
Where the Orson Welles Movie Theater used to be,
From which in former days you faintly heard
The voices of the great dead stars still vying
In rich complaint, or else in exaltation
Of meeting or farewell, in rituals
Of wit o'ermastered, or in ecstasy
Of woe beyond the experience of saints.

In the alley between the yard and the old theater
The wildman is, covered with leaves or clad
In the bark of our indigenous flourishing trees,
Elaborately enscrolled and decorated
With the names of heavenly pity; there he sleeps
In the freedom of his distress among abandoned
Containers of paint, eggshell and offwhite tincts,
Both raw and burnt, vermilion, pinks, and rose,
Purples, and blues, and other hues and shades,
Close by the tangled roll of wire screening,
Under a scribbled hieroglyphic sign.

The Blind People

– Baudelaire, "Les Aveugles"

What is the difference between the unlimited
Blackness they walk in this ridiculous
Fashion through, and the eternal silence?
The sounds of the city, with all its laughter and music,
Are a denial I walk through with my stupid
Questions when I look at them. What are they
Looking up at the sky for, with such blind
Scrutinizing? Just think about them. How foolish,
And terrible, they look; weird; sleepwalkers;
Puppets on a string, the divine light gone
Forever from their eyes; and still they keep on
Staring up at the sky; they never bow
Their dreaming heads in noble meditation
Over the pavements of the raucous city.

The Proselyte

A man the unclean spirits had gotten into
Got into the parish hall on Tuesday night.

The unclean spirits poured out through his skin
In the form of filth and cried out in that form,

And cried out in the form of how he went
Rapidly back and forth as if on many

Errands to one person and another
Or to nobody, up and down the parish hall,

Little trips back and forward rapidly,
Like a wasp or fly, hysterical with purpose,

Battering himself against our difference.
There was authority in him as he went

Carrying his message to one of us and another.
Who had condemned him to this filth and to

This unavailing rage? And the little voice
Crying out something in the body's cage?

The voice was pitifully small, as if
From someplace else or time of childhood, say,

Or country other, telling us something no one
In the parish hall could possibly understand,

Rabbinical, as if of ancient learning
Knowledgeable, and unintelligible,

A proselyte, the morphemes were uncouth.
His body was clad in the black of the unclean spirits.

The Proselyte

And then he was gone away from the dining room,
A wasp trapped in a house, desperately trying,

Flying from one room into another room,
How to get out of the place in which it was,

Or else to carry the message to some place other.
He went to the phone on the wall of the hall outside

And said into the phone whatever it was he was saying,
And tore the phone out of the wall and talked to the wall,

Telling it things in the tiny faroff doleful
Insect crying voice in that other language.

And then he went to the outside door and said
To the outside door of the parish hall whatever

It was he said to us and the phone and the wall;
And then he was gone away into the night.

Johnson on Pope

– from The Lives of the Poets

He was protuberant behind, before;
Born beautiful, he had grown up a spider;
Stature so low, he could not sit at table
Like taller men; in middle life so feeble
He could not dress himself, nor stand upright
Without a canvas bodice; in the long night
Made servants peevish with his demands for coffee;
Trying to make his spider's legs less skinny,
He wore three pairs of stockings, which a maid
Had to draw on and off; one side was contracted,
But his face was not displeasing, his eyes were vivid.

At the Street Corner

– after Rilke, "Das Lied des Zwerges"

Maybe my soul's all right.
But my body's all wrong,
All bent and twisted,
It's this that hurts me so.

My soul keeps trying, trying
To straighten my body up.
It hangs on my skeleton, frantic,
Flapping its terrified wings.

Look here, look at my hands,
They look like little wet toads
After a rainstorm's over,
Hopping, hopping, hopping.

Maybe God didn't like
The look of my face when He saw it.
Sometimes a big dog
Looks right into it.

The License Plate

On the way back from the hospital we saw
A message on the license plate of a car.

It said GOD HAS. Has what?
Decided finally what to do about it?

The answer to the question that you asked?
The whole world in His Hands? Fucked up? Again?

Apologized? Failed to apologize?
The car went on its way ahead of us.

The Late-Hour Poem

In an hour of furious clarity,
By liquor made,
Full of a fierce charity,
My harp I played!

I made a loud uproar!
I went in turn
From door to every door.
Marry or burn!

Love your neighbor! I cried.
Pity the poor
Divided people, who side
By side here lie,

Transfixed in sleep; and shadow
Covers each eye!
On house and house the echo
Rang and rebounded.

My harp made everybody know
How brave I sounded!

At a Bar

While in a bar I bore
Indignity with those
Others whose hearts were sore
Or sour or sick or such
As made them humankind,
I looked into my glass
To see if I could find
Something to give me ease.

Narcissus at the pool,
I looked lovingly at
My own disordered fool,
Who would not tell me much.
But stared patiently back.
He would not tell me what
I'd ever have or lack
He would not tell me that.

I looked along the bar
And saw my fellow creature
Bravely standing there.
"By word, sign, or touch,"
I cried, in my mute heart,
"Tell me, be my teacher,
Be learnèd in that art,
What is my name and nature?"

My pulse ticked in my wrist;
The noon hung around unawares;
Outside the traffic passed.
Like quiet cattle or such,
Standing about a pool,
Dumb ignorant creatures,
My fellow, my self, my fool,
Ignorant of our natures.

To Varus

– Horace, Ode i.18

For planting in the rich Tiburtine soil
Upon the slopes of Mt. Catillus, Varus,
Favor no plant before the sacred vine.
Bacchus commands that everything be hard
For him who abstains from wine, and Bacchus says
The troubles that wear away our days are not
Made easier by any other means.
After a drink or two who is it who
Complains about the hardships of his lot –
His poverty, or his service in the army?
Who fails to praise you then, O father Bacchus?
Who fails to praise you too, O queen of love?
And yet there is a lesson in the example
Of the fight between the Centaurs and the Lapiths,
That went so far too far at the drunken banquet.
And there's another in the Sithonian drinkers
Who think they tell right from wrong by squinting along
The disappearing line libidinous desire
Draws on the wet bartop. I would not dare
To stir you up, O Bacchus, against your will,
Nor will I be the one to betray to the light
The secret signs that you have covered over
In grape and ivy leaves. Bacchus, repress
The cymbal and the Berecynthian horn
And those who revel in that raucous music:
Blind Love that has no eyes but for itself;
Vain Glory with its vacant head held high;
And barfly Faithlessness whose promiscuous tongue
Spills all its secrets into promiscuous ears.

After Edward Hopper: Somebody in a Bar

The veined hand like a stitched glove
On the bar left lying;
The bold brow, bald, bare
To the bare bulb's black glare;
Slope-shouldered, unready;

This starer into the mirror
Over the bar; this mirror
The transformer into horror,
Into terror of what whose habit is
To be by daylight pain

Merely; dull repeater; drudger;
Trudger on the treadmill of the nerves;
The innocence of animals drinks here,
Here at this lonely pool the poor beast drinks.

Coffee Lips

The guest who came in to the street people's suppers last night,
An elderly man with a lost smart little boy's face and a look

As if he might turn against you anytime soon,
As if he'd just come into this world and he was extremely

Wary about what the world was going to be, and he said,
"If I ask you a question will you give me a truthful answer?"

And I said, "That depends on what the question is,"
Thinking the little elderly boy looked sophisticated and

As if he'd in fact been a long time in the world
And would get the tone right, and maybe he did, or maybe he didn't;

At any rate he went on to ask the question,
"When I come into places like this and there are people holding

Coffee cups to their lips and they look at me,
Are they about to drink the coffee or not to drink the coffee?"

He was balancing the world on the tip of his witty unknowing nose.
I felt like I was falling down someplace else than anywhere there.

Song of the Drunkard

– Rilke, "Das Lied des Trinkers"

I don't know what it was I wanted to hold onto.
I kept losing it and I didn't know what it was
Except I wanted to hold onto it. The drink kept it in,
So at least for awhile it felt as if I had it,
Whatever it was. But it was the drink that had it
And held it and had hold of me too. Asshole.

Now I'm a card in the drink's hand while he keeps smiling
Like he doesn't give a shit in a game that's going badly,
And when death wins he'll scratch his scabby neck
With the greasy card and throw me down on the table
And then I'll just be another one of the cards
In the pile on the fucking table. So what the fuck.

Incubus

– at the supper for street people

The young man who comes all muffled up from harm,
With whatever he has found, newspaper pages
Carefully folded to make a weirdly festive
Hat or hood, down almost over his eyes.

Everything carefully arranged to make him other.
The paper covered razorblade in his mouth,
Or the bit of wood, like carrying a message.
A fantasy so clever, outwitting itself,

That it became what it was he was, and so
He was what it was. The long loose shirt too big
For him, the pantaloons too big for him,
Loose like the pantaloons of the circus clown,

Some kind of jacket too big, he got it somewhere.
His burden slept dreaming everywhere upon him,
As if his whole body and the clothes he wore dreamed
Of his condition and the dream came true.

His clothes slept on him as if they were his lover.

Movie Star Peter at the Supper for Street People

The style a form of concealment the way style is.
His manners seemed a parody, almost,
Of manners, a movie star of bygone days;

Strangely elaborate, highly stylized manners,
Complicit with his fame and with your praise;
Looking towards you and then away from you,

Star-like, movie-star like, a dance routine,
The walk almost a glide, or elegant shuffle,
Always on the verge of veering away,

Circling away and over to the other side
Of the frozen skating arena that he was on;
A dancer's courtesy, the courtesy,

I mean, of the dancer to the audience,
Flirtatious and familiar, only for you,
And entirely impersonal and withheld.

All of the above, though, maybe, misses the point,
Because it seems to say he knew about
What he was doing or what the style was for,

And nothing let one be sure that this was so;
A look on his face of amusement, as if he knew
A secret that he shared with you and yet

Kept to himself, as if it only showed
The cryptogram but wouldn't provide the key
To read it with. But could he read the code?

One night, late at night, as we were driving
Home from having had dinner out, in Boston,
We saw him figure skating through Charles Street Circle,

Movie Star Peter at the Supper for Street People

Right through and among the circling lights of cars
As if with champion skill on thin ice whirling
Oblivious to the astonished blaring horns,

As a dancer or skater seems, while dancing to
The music that we hear, oblivious to
The music that we hear and listening to

Some other music heard from somewhere else.
So Peter moved like a dancer or skater through
And among the dangerous outraged cars as if

Untouchable and untouched and moving to
The sounds of something else from somewhere else –
The music maybe of his madness was it?

It was as if he skated in solitude
And glided whirling on a lonely tarn
Far out away from everything there is.

Wallenda

– *i.m. Arthur Gold*

I saw him in a coffee shop in Cambridge,
Radiant, argumentative, talking away
As joyful as anything, terrified, dying,
Sisyphus in a panic, the words pushing
The joy ahead of him like a stone up hill;
Or else he was like a bicycle racer racing,
Faster and faster racing what he was saying,
Because in what he was saying no matter what,
He couldn't get out ahead of the sniggering voice
He kept on hearing whispering under his talking,
Telling him what was going to happen to him;
Or else he was standing out on the edge of a cliff
Trying his best to shout into the wind
That was blowing hard in against him from the planets;
Or else he was "carrying a twenty-three-foot
Balancing-pole and he moved out smoothly onto
The three-quarters-of-an-inch-thick cable one-
Hundred-and-twenty-feet high, beginning his
Seven-hundred-and-fifty-foot walk. The weather was bright
Cold and windy. He continued to move out smoothly
Until he reached the midpoint. Then suddenly
The wind picked up to thirty miles per hour.
He leaned into the wind to lean against it.
The wire was `dancing' now under his feet.
`Sit down, sit down,' one of his family called.
He semi-crouched and called out down to the nine
Men who were working the guy wires down below,
`Tighten it, tighten it.' DAREDEVIL. Then he tried
To grab the cable but could not hold it and then
Put both hands back on the pole and silently
Daredevil Wallenda fell plummeting down to death."

Reading Arthur Gold's Poem "Chest Cancer"

A flash of somber red
Against the Maine-drenched green,
Back of the Victory Garden,
As we kids crouched under the sun,
Weeding. It was the only sight of fox
I ever had. In the Jersey winter
I thought ah if I could have held
That fox in my line of sight. ...

On our way to have my septum removed
My father told me of the foxcub and
The Spartan boy. He meant to encourage.

I was guilty of telling the same cruel tale
To the same end, to my little girl Anna,
Who when it was over and done with asked
What did the Spartans have against pets.

But afterwards in the car when I complained
Of the hurt he held me against his chest.
So Anna holds her cat Rosette.

These memories and imaginations
Gnaw at my repose.

Anna's tenderness to Rosette,
My dad's flash of tenderness to me:
Paradise would be if I could hold them
Before not behind my eyes.

– AG

"Before not behind my eyes." One thing about it
Is that the lines were written with the knowledge
That except perhaps in having the thought and also
Perhaps in writing it down in lines in a poem

Reading Arthur Gold's Poem "Chest Cancer"

There is no Paradise behind the eyes;
And soon there would not be "before," "behind."
The thought, the line of verse, is the repose,
In which the idea of Paradise still is.

Some Paradise. Some repose. But these
Memories and imaginations that are
The way the idea of Paradise is held
Are also the fox that gnaws in the breast of repose,

Even while Arthur's carried in the father's bosom,
The bosom of Abraham. Clearly Arthur
Is also thinking of the Akedah,
In the tangle of family feeling, the cruelty,

Inadvertent and loving, which at the same time
Seems to be part of the natural scheme of things,
The tender well-meant ill-judging cruelty,
The father's story of the Spartan child,

Then Arthur's telling the story to his child.
The father telling that story is Abraham
Driving Isaac his son down to the doctor's office,
Faithful to the laws of how things are,

Except that in this poem instead of the ram
Caught in the branches there to save Isaac's life,
There is the sighting of the fox that summer,
The cancer, the bosom friend, behind the garden.

In our consenting, by the ways we spend
Our days obeying the laws of how things are,
We deliver up each other unto the God
Until one day no ram is caught in the thicket.

Reading Arthur Gold's "Trolley Poem"

> *Do you*
> *Remember slow-moving trolleys?*
> *Do you remember men dropping*
> *From the rear-end platforms*
> *Of slow-moving trolleys?*
> *So our faith in God slowly*
> *Drops but not the monkey*
> *On our backs, not his nails*
> *Digging into our necks:*
> *Guilt, justice, the desire*
> *To be good.*
> *Is There No End?*
>
> *– AG*

God, lights flashing, bells ringing, God on his tracks,
Heading away somewhere, to some destination.

Who were the people who managed to get on board?
Where is it they were being taken to?

Arthur, yes, I remember the slow-moving trolleys;
I remember the men clinging on to the trolleys,

Clinging like monkeys not just to rear-end platforms
But hanging on by their nails just under the cables

That hooked up above to the flashing sparking lines.
A lot of fireworks, God, on your way to some station,

Rattling and clanging, making a lot of noise.
One thing you're famous for is making noise.

Then, suddenly, in the poem, God is the monkey
That rides us like the habit we can't get free of,

Reading Arthur Gold's "Trolley Poem"

And for Arthur in his extremity not being able
To free himself from virtue was part of the pain;

The obligations of being what he was,
Father, and teacher, setting some kind of example.

My sister Penny at my niece's house,
The day her blood reported that the cancer

Had intensified ten times since the last report.
The obligation of being who she was,

Listening to the family pleasantries
With something like what seemed to be like pleasure.

Reading Arthur Gold's Poem "On the Beach at Asbury"

I lie half asleep on the beach at Asbury.
The hairs on my father's chest are little tendrils of death.
The sun beating down, the murmur and susurrus of voices,
Prices of this and that, who's in, who's out, the stockmarket,
    boys' names, girls',
And behind or below the comforting murmur, faintly,
    disturbed by cries,
The other clamor of the beating surf,
Felt somehow, heard somehow, through the warm sand
    and in my body as I bake
    all this comes back to me now,
But especially the intricate mess of black, gray, white hair
    on my father's sundarkened chest,
    Not seen or touched but known,
And the sense of something coming, something dire,
    hidden below or behind it all.

– AG

Arthur knew perfectly well that this derives
From Whitman one of his fathers, and the hair
On his father's chest is the beautiful uncut hair,
The grass, that grows on graves; knew perfectly well
That in this poem he was "lying half-asleep"
In Abraham's bosom; and knew the fantasy
Of Lear that in Paradise he and his daughter
Would tell each other stories who's in who's out
And witness together the comedy of the pageant
Of lords and ladies as they pass below.
The beauty of it is that the verse proceeds,
Knowing these things, as if it didn't know them,
So "stockmarket" comes in easy, boys' names, girls' names,
The family conversation on the beach,
Everything made of common materials –
There isn't a person brought up near the ocean
Who hasn't heard around him as he lay

In safety in the family conversation,
Half-hearing it all around him, sheltered in it,
Sleeping in sunshine as if asleep in heaven,
The sound of the all-embracing sea coming in,
And that's what Arthur's poem hears all around it.
But in the last line of Arthur's poem the penultimate word
Is "it," and "it" refers, as I read it, to
The word "something," and back beyond that, his father's "chest,"
And back beyond that, the clamoring sound of the "surf."
Our death is in the beating of the surf,
"The waters of the earth gathering upon us,"
And in the beating of our father's heart,
The beating heart in Abraham's bosom, on which
There grows the beautiful grass that grows on graves.
Death's heartbeat beats in every line of the poem

Old People

Their old skin has the marks in it of the sea.
The patterns of waves. Traces of sand crabs in the patterns.
Wind traces. Splinters of seashells. Markings of kelpfronds.

Their voices are loud against the waves coming in.
They shout out into the wind that blows back into
Their mouths the words they are trying to shout out into

The wind that blows against them. What they possess
They possess with a fierceness that comes from a deafness that isn't
Deaf, but it hears the waves saying, "Take them, take them."

But they cry out against the waves in voices
Violent and weak, "I won't give in to them."
They're in a room full of people almost without

Any furniture, only some metal chairs,
So the walls resound and Cerberus barks a lot.
It is a nightmare of the high school lunchroom.

Soul

What am I doing inside this old man's body?
I feel like I'm the insides of a lobster,
All thought, and all digestion, and pornographic
Inquiry, and getting about, and bewilderment,
And fear, avoidance of trouble, belief in what,
God knows, vague memories of friends, and what
They said last night, and seeing, outside of myself,
From here inside myself, my waving claws
Inconsequential, wavering, and my feelers
Preternatural, trembling, with their amazing
Troubling sensitivity to threat;
And I'm aware of and embarrassed by my ways
Of getting around, and my protective shell.
Where is it that she I loved has gone, as this
Cold sea water's washing over my back?

x

Adapted From the Bannatyne Manuscript

Of love and truth with long continuance,
    Let others learn from what my love has taught me;
All you who study how to turn away
    From the governance of love, come learn from me
All that the course of faithful love has brought me,
    Than whom there never was whose heart was surer
Of what it knows and holds, since first I saw her.

Neither for joy, nor sharp adversity,
    Nor for disdain, dread, danger, or despair,
For life, for death, for woe, for destiny,
    For bliss, for bale, for comfort, or for care,
For chance of fortune, turning here and there,
    From her shall never turn my plain heart true,
Whatever I suffer of sorrow, old or new.

My married heart shall never turn from her
    Unto another so long as my five wits
Shall last, whose whole consent is given to her
    Until death's rage shall cleave me to the root.
So shall I love her ever, in spite of what-
    Soever circumstance can do to us.
God grant I go to the grave before she goes.

Aubade

If the early morning were like the dewy steaming
Rising of cloudy brightness
Out of the shadowy gardens of this sleep;
Were like this long last night's last dream, unquenched,
Drifting from the eye's
Opening splendor on the day's first instant;
Oh if the early morning
The slight smoke were of the banked fire of the sleeping
Ardor I watched so long,
So long heard breathe in the heart of the heart's easy
Selfhood, knowing nothing but its sleeping:
Then were the morning one
Creature of your body's dear awakening.

In Eden

You lie in our bed as if an orchard were over us,

You are what's fallen from those fatal boughs.

Where will we go when they send us away from here?

Orpheus and Eurydice

– Virgil, Georgics, *IV, ii. 457-527*

                         ... She fled from you,
Headlong along the river, unhappy maiden,
And did not see the frightful snake that lurked
In the high grass, guarding the riverbank.
The cries of the sister band of Dryads filled
The air as high as the mountain-tops; the cliffs
Of Rhodope wept, the cliffs of Pangaea wept,
And the warrior land of the Getae, Oríthyia, Hebrus.
Alone upon the unfrequented shore
Orpheus, playing his lyre, sang to himself
His songs of you, dear wife, as day came on
With the light of the morning sun, and as the light
Descended in the evening. Singing he went
Down through the very throat of Táenarus,
The high gate of the dark kingdom of Dis,
And through the murky grove where Terror dwells
In black obscurity, and entered into
The Mane's place, the place of the dreadful King
And the hearts no human prayers can cause to pity.

And, set in motion by the sound of music,
From the lowest depths of Erebus there came,
As numerous as the many hundred birds
That, driven there by the coming on of evening
Or by a winter storm, fly in for shelter
In the foliage of a grove, the flittering shades,
The unsubstantial phantom shapes of those
For whom there is not any light at all –
Women and men, famous great-hearted heroes,
The life in their hero bodies now defunct,
Unmarried boys and girls, sons whom their fathers
Had had to watch being placed on the funeral pyre,
And all around them the hideous tangling reeds
And the black ooze of Cocytos' swampy waters;
Nine times Styx wound its fettering chain around them.

And the house of Death was spellbound by his music,
All the way down to the bottom of Tartarus;
Spellbound the snakes in the hair of the Furies too;
And Cérberus the Hell-Dog's all three mouths
Were open-mouthed and silent, forgetting to bark;
The wind was still, and Ixíon's wheel stopped turning.

And now, as he was carefully going back
The way he came, and step by step avoiding
All possible wrong steps, and step by step
Eurýdice, whom he was bringing back,
Unseen behind his back was following –
For this is what Proserpina had commanded –
They were coming very near the upper air,
And a sudden madness seized him, madness of love,
A madness to be forgiven if Hell but knew
How to forgive; he stopped in his tracks, and then,
Just as they were just about to emerge
Out into the light, suddenly, seized by love,
Bewildered into heedlessness, alas!,
His purpose overcome, he turned, and looked
Back at Eurydice! And then and there
His labor was spilled and flowed away like water.
The implacable tyrant broke the pact: three times
The pools of Avérnus heard the sound of thunder.

"What was it," she cried, "what madness, Orpheus, was it,
That has destroyed us, you and me, oh look!
The cruel Fates already call me back,
And sleep is covering over my swimming eyes.
Farewell; I'm being carried off into
The vast surrounding dark and reaching out
My strengthless hands to you forever more
Alas not yours." And saying this, like smoke
Disintegrating into air she was
Dispersed away and vanished from his eyes

And never saw him again, and he was left
Clutching at shadows, with so much still to say.
And the boatman never again would take him across
The barrier of the marshy waters of Hell.
What could he do? His wife twice taken from him.
How could he bear it? How could his tears move Hell?
The Stygian boat has carried her away.

*

And, it is said, that he, day after day,
For seven months beside the river Strymon,
Sat underneath a towering cliff, and wept,
And sang, and told in song his story; entranced,
The wild beasts listened; entranced, the oak trees moved
Closer to hear the song, which was like that
Of the nightingale, in the shade of a poplar tree,
In mourning for her children who were taken,
As yet unfledged, by a herdsman, hard of heart,
Who had happened upon the nest – she weeps all night
And over and over repeats her lamentation
And fills the listening air with her sad complaint.

No thought of marriage or any other love
Could turn his heart away from its bereavement.
Alone he roamed the Hyperborean North
And wandered along the snowy banks of the Don
Or through the barren frozen fields on the sides
Of Riphaean mountains, in grief for his lost wife
And Hades' empty promise, until the enraged
Cicónian Bacchantes, in a nocturnal
Ritual orgy, tore his body to pieces
And scattered the pieces everywhere, far and wide;
And as his head, cut off from his marble neck,
Was tumbling down the rushing course of the Hebrus,
His voice and tongue, with his last breath, cried out,

"Eurydice! O poor Eurydice!"
And the banks of the downward river Hebrus echoed
"Eurydice! O poor Eurydice!"

Lake Water

It is a summer afternoon in October.
I am sitting on a wooden bench, looking out
At the lake through a tall screen of evergreens,
Or rather, looking out across the plane of the lake,
Seeing the light shaking upon the water
As if it were a shimmering of heat.
Yesterday, when I sat here, it was the same,
The same displaced out-of-season effect.
Seen twice it seemed a truth was being told.
Some of the trees I can see across the lake
Have begun to change, but it is as if the air
Had entirely given itself over to summer,
With the intention of denying its own proper nature.
There is a breeze perfectly steady and persistent
Blowing in toward shore from the other side
Or from the world beyond the other side.
The mild sound of the little tapping waves
The breeze has caused – there's something infantile
About it, a baby at the breast. The light
Is moving and not moving upon the water.

The breeze picks up slightly but still steadily,
The increase in the breeze becomes the mild
Dominant event, compelling with sweet oblivious
Authority alterations in light and shadow,
Alterations in the light of the sun on the water,
Which becomes at once denser and more quietly
Excited, like a concentration of emotions
That had been dispersed and scattered and now were not.
Then there's the mitigation of a cloud,
And the light subsides a little, as if into itself.
Although this is a lake it is as if
A tide were running mildly into shore.
The sound of the water so softly battering
Against the shore is decidedly sexual,
In its liquidity, its regularity,

Lake Water

Its persistence, its infantile obliviousness.
It is as if it had come back to being
A beginning, an origination of life.

The plane of the water is like a page on which
Phrases and even sentences are written,
But because of the breeze, and the turning of the year,
And the sense that this lake water, as it is being
Experienced on a particular day, comes from
Some source somewhere, beneath, within, itself,
Or from somewhere else, nearby, a spring, a brook,
Its pure origination somewhere else,
It is like an idea for a poem not yet written
And maybe never to be completed, because
The surface of the page is like lake water,
That takes back what is written on its surface,
And all my language about the lake and its
Emotions or its sweet obliviousness,
Or even its being like an origination,
Is all erased with the changing of the breeze
Or because of the heedless passing of a cloud.

When, moments after she died, I looked into her face,
It was as untelling as something natural,
A lake, say, the surface of it unreadable,
Its sources of meaning unfindable anymore.
Her mouth was open as if she had something to say;
But maybe my saying so is a figure of speech.

The White Skunk

That glorious morning late in August when
The rosy-fingered dawn had scattered shadows
Away from the dreams I had dreamed the night before,
I looked out the back door of my condo, seeing
The parking lot we share, the cars we own,
And the houses all around, an embracing scene,
And there was Manfred and his small child Julia,
And, I thought for a moment, a little white toy
Trundling along behind her on its wheels.
But something was wrong with this. Julia, though little,
Wasn't so little as to be trundling such
A toy as what I thought I was seeing there,
On that glorious morning late in August when
The rosy-fingered dawn had scattered shadows.

And then I saw that the toy I thought I saw
Was not a toy but a little white skunk intently
Following Julia's legs and studying them,
And then, of course, her father had snatched her up
Into his arms, and was backing away from the skunk,
And kicking at it to get it away, but the skunk
Kept following, it seemed for a very long time,
As the three of them kept on this way on their way,
Julia crying now, a piercing cry,
And Manfred perplexed, a father protecting his child,
Backing away and saying, in a voice
Carefully calm and maybe pretending to be
Almost amused, "What should I do about this?"
Holding his child in his arms, having to keep
Backing away, unable to turn his back
On this bizarre studious creature following them.
Transfixed in the doorway of the place I live in
I stood there out of time, watching them go.

But then, as they were halfway down the driveway
The creature turned aside and disappeared

The White Skunk

Into the tall grass alongside the driveway,
And Manfred, carrying Julia, was able to turn
And quickly make his way away from there
To the pre-school across the street from the end of the driveway.
A moment later the skunk appeared again
And ran across the lawn beside our house,
Intently studying the ground, near-sighted
Creature reading the ground for information,
Moving about the yard between our house
And the kindred house next door, purposeful, wandering.
What was it trying to find? Where was it going? –

A reader of the ground as if it were
The walls of the facility at Mount Auburn
Where she kept wandering the halls, reading blank walls
To see if there was an exit there, or maybe
A bulletin board telling her what to do,
Telling her how to be there, or where to be,
Or what she was trying to find, or where she was going,
Intently studying where it was she was.

The skunk was white where a skunk is normally black,
And striped black where it's normally striped white.
Was it transmogrified.? Come up from down there
In the Underworld where it could have been changed like that?
It came back over across the lawn towards where
I was standing transfixed in the doorway of my dwelling,
Its eyes still intently studying the ground,
Close reader of the text whose narrative
Or whose instruction it was following.

Orpheus, I, stepped back in nameless fear,
As it looked as if the skunk was reading its way
Towards the back porch steps up into my condominium,
Coming towards me as if it were coming home.
And then the skunk ran past my back porch steps

The White Skunk

Reading the ground, paying no heed to me,
And disappeared in the groundcover we planted
To ornament the door yard of our dwelling
In the world the strange white skunk had disappeared from.

On the River Bank

Virgil, Aeneid, *VI, ii. 297-330*

From here there is a road which leads to where
The waters of Tartarean Acheron are,
Where a bottomless whirlpool thick with muck
Heaves and seethes and vomits mire into
The river Cocytos. Here is the dreadful boatman,
Who keeps these waters, frightful in his squalor,
Charon, the gray hairs of his unkempt beard
Depending from his chin, his glaring eyes
On fire, his filthy mantle hanging by
A loose knot from his shoulders. All by himself
He manages the sails and with his pole
Conveys the dead across in his dark boat –
He's old, but, being a god, old age is young.

A vast crowd, so many, rushed to the river bank,
Women and men, famous great-hearted heroes,
The life in their hero bodies now defunct,
Unmarried boys and girls, sons whom their fathers
Had had to watch being placed on the funeral pyre;
As many as the leaves of the forest that,
When autumn's first chill comes, fall from the branches;
As many as the birds that flock in to the land
From the great deep when, the season, turning cold,
Has driven them over the seas to seek the sun,
They stood beseeching on the river bank,
Yearning to be the first to be carried across,
Stretching their hands out towards the farther shore.
But the stern ferryman, taking only this one
Or this other one, pushes the rest away.
Aeneas cries out, excited by the tumult,
"O virgin, why are they crowding at the river?
What is it that the spirits want? What is it
That decides why some of them are pushed away
And others sweep across the livid waters?"
The aged priestess thus: "Anchises' son,

True scion of the gods, these are the pools
Of the river Cocytos and this the Stygian marsh,
Whose power it is to make the gods afraid
Not to keep their word. All in this crowd are helpless
Because their bodies have not been covered over.
The boatman that you see is Charon. Those
Who are being carried across with him are they
Who have been buried. It is forbidden
To take any with him across the echoing waters
That flow between these terrible riverbanks
Who have not found a resting-place for their bones.
Restlessly to and fro along these shores
They wander waiting for a hundred years.
Not until after that, the longed-for crossing."

That Now Are Wild and Do Not Remember

Where did you go to, when you went away?
It is as if you step by step were going
Someplace elsewhere into some other range
Of speaking, that I had no gift for speaking,
Knowing nothing of the language of that place
To which you went with naked foot at night
Into the wilderness there elsewhere in the bed,
Somewhere else in the house beyond my seeking.
I have been so dislanguaged by what happened,
I cannot speak the words that somewhere you
Maybe were speaking to others where you went.
Maybe they talk together where they are,
Restlessly wandering along the shore,
Waiting for a way to cross the river.

Untitled Dream Poem

What are the plants that blossom in the dark?
In my liminal dreaming waking it was green grapes
On tangled vines where some of the grapes had ripened
Nocturnally red and looking like and being

The red rear lights of cars rushing away,
To get to the shore to try to get onto the boat,
And the rustle of the garments of the dead
Was the rustle of the bed sheets on the bed,

The rustle of the wandering where, the blankness
Of the faces where they meet in restaurants saying
Things to one another that do not reach
Across the tabletops, the buried dead,

Unburied till we forget them who they were.
When Adam asked the angel how they did it,
The angel blushed, his face was rosy red,
So something went on there that we can't have.

XI

Resemblance

It was my father in that restaurant
On Central Avenue in Orange, New Jersey,
Where I stopped for lunch and a drink, after coming away
From visiting, after many years had passed,
The place to which I'd brought my father's ashes
And the ashes of my mother, and where my father's
Grandparents, parents, brothers, had been buried,
And others of the family, all together.

The atmosphere was smoky, and there was a vague
Struggling transaction going on between
The bright day light of the busy street outside,
And the somewhat dirty light of the unwashed
Ceiling globes of the restaurant I was in.
He was having lunch. I couldn't see what he was having
But he seemed to be eating, though maybe without
Noticing whatever it was he may have been eating;
He seemed to be listening to a conversation
With two or three others – Shades of the Dead come back
From where they went to when they went away? –
Or maybe those others weren't speaking at all? Maybe
It was a dumbshow? Put on for my benefit?

It was the eerie persistence of his not
Seeming to recognize that I was there,
Watching him from my table across the room;
It was also the sense of his being included
In the conversation around him, and yet not,
Though this in life had been familiar to me,
No great change from what had been there before,
Even in my sense that I, across the room,
Was excluded, which went along with my sense of him
When he was alive, that often he didn't feel
Included in the scenes and talk around him,
And his isolation itself excluded others.

Resemblance

Where were we, in that restaurant that day?
Had I gone down into the world of the dead?
Were those other people really Shades of the Dead?
We expect that, if they came back, they would come back
To impart some knowledge of what it was they had learned.
Or if this was, indeed, Down There, then they,
Down there, would reveal, to us who visit them,
In a purified language some truth that in our condition
Of being alive we are unable to know.

Their tongues are ashes when they'd speak to us.

Is it because there is a silence we
Are all of us *forbidden* to cross, not only
The silence that divides the dead from the living,
But, antecedent to that, the silence that
There is between the living and the living,
Unable to reach across that silence through
The baffling light? Among the living the body
Is able to do so, sometimes, and that is a good,
But the mind, constricted, inhibited by its ancestral
Knowledge of final separation, holds back,
Unable to complete what it wanted to say.

What is your name that I can call you by?

Virgil said, when Eurydice died again,
"There was still so much to say" that had not been said
Even before her first death from which he had vainly
Attempted, with his singing, to rescue her.

Scrim

I sit here in a shelter behind the words
Of what I'm writing, looking out as if
Through a dim curtain of rain, that keeps me in here.
The words are like a scrim upon a page,
Obscuring what might be there beyond the scrim.
I can dimly see there's something or someone there.

But I can't tell if it's God, or one of his angels,
Or the past, or future, or who it is I love,
My mother or father lost, or my lost sister,

Or my wife lost when I was too late to get there,
I only know that there's something, or somebody, there.
Tell me your name. How was it that I knew you?

Ancestral Lines

It's as when following the others' lines,
Which are the tracks of somebody gone before,
Leaving me mischievous clues, telling me who

They were and who it was they weren't,
And who it is I am because of them,
Or, just for the moment, reading them, I am,

Although the next moment I'm back in myself, and lost.
My father at the piano saying to me,
"Listen to this, he called the piece *Warum*?"

And the nearest my father could come to saying what
He made of that was lamely to say he didn't,
Schumann didn't, my father didn't, know why.

"What's in a dog's heart"? I once asked in a poem,
And Christopher Ricks when he read it said, "Search me."
He wasn't just being funny, of course; he was right.

You can't tell anything much about who you are
By exercising on the Romantic bars.
What *are* the wild waves saying? I don't know.

And Shelley didn't know, and knew he didn't.
In his great poem, "Ode to the West Wind," he
Said that the leaves of his pages were blowing away,

Dead leaves, like ghosts from an enchanter fleeing.

Everybody's Tree

The storm broke over us on a summer night,
All brilliance and display; and being out,
Dangerously I thought, on the front porch standing,
Over my head the lightning skated and blistered
And sizzled and skidded and yelled in the bursting down
Around my maybe fourteen-years-old being,
And in spite of all the fireworks up above
And what you'd thought would have been the heat of all
That exuberant rage, the air was suddenly cool
And fresh and as peaceable as could be,
Down on the porch, so different from what it was
My body was expecting. The raindrops on
The front porch railing arms peacefully dripped
As if they weren't experiencing what
Was coming down from above them as an outrage.
My body could reinterpret it as a blessing,
Being down there in the cool beneath the heat.
It wasn't of course being blessed but being suddenly
Singled out with a sense of being a being.

Sometime early on in the nineteenth century
Down in the part of New Jersey called New Sweden,
Someone with some familial link to me,
Maybe a grandsire down a maternal line,
Whose name was Isaiah Toy, was sitting up
In the house of his dying bachelor uncle, who
Was also Isaiah Toy, and Isaiah Toy,
His uncle, would leave his farm to Isaiah Toy,
His nephew, who was sitting in a chair
In the next room to where his uncle was dying.
I don't know what kind of light it would have been
That he was reading the Bible by while his uncle
Slept towards leaving the farm to him, when suddenly,
Reading, who was it, Matthew, or maybe Mark,
The glory of the Lord broke over his head,

Or so he said. Methodists got excited when
In the woods of their confusion suddenly
The moonlight burst above their heads and they
Were ever after then enlightened beings.

"Light suddenly broke upon his mind. For fear
Of disturbing his dying uncle with his joy,
The expression of which he could not repress, he went
Out of the house into the brilliant moonlight
Shining upon the snow, and gave vent to his feelings,
Shouting "Glory to God! Glory to God in the Highest!"

Coming back in from the porch, while the storm went on
Above our little house, I went to close the window
Of the dining room that looked out back of the house
And I could see, could dimly see, the backs
Of the Bowdoin Street houses all in a row,
Occasionally lit up and washed blank by
Downpours of the lightning of the storm:
The Beckers' house, the Gileses' house, the Demarests',
Jean Williams's where she lay in "the sleeping-sickness,"
And Bessie Phelps's house, the one next to hers,
The property lines of the houses and their yards
Made briefly briefly clear by the lightning flashing.
Running along the back of the hither yards
Was a tiny ditch defining the property lines
Between where our Yale Street backyards ended
And where the yonder Bowdoin Street houses' backyards
Backed up to it; my childhood fantasy thought
The waterless tiny ditch was the vestige of
A mysterious long ago bygone vanished river
That came from somewhere else and went somewhere.
I don't know, didn't know, though of course I knew them,
Whatever went on in those houses, or in my mind,
Or my mother's mind, or my father's, asleep upstairs,
Though I kept wondering, and wonder still,

What is it they were doing? Who were they?
All, all, are gone, the unfamiliar faces.

Over beyond in the night there was a houseless
Wooded lot next door to Bessie's house;
Because of the houselessness and because of the trees,
I could think of it as a forest like the forest
In Hawthorne's great short story Young Goodman Brown,
And from out that window looking out at the back
I could faintly see, or thought I could see,
Maybe once or twice, by a flash, a raining gust
Of the light of lightning, the waving tops of trees
In that empty wooded lot beyond Bessie's house.
The houseless tiny lot seemed like a forest
And in the forest there was a certain tree
Which all of us children somehow knew was known
As Everybody's Tree, so it was called,
Though nobody knew who it was who gave it its name;
And on the smooth hide of its trunk there were initials,
Nobody knew who it was who had inscribed them.
We children had never gathered around that tree
To show each other our bodies. I remember how,
Crossing through that houseless wooded lot
On my way home on an autumn afternoon,
That strange tree, with the writing on it, seemed
Ancient, a totem, a rhapsody playing a music
Written according to an inscrutable key.
How did I ever know what the tree was called?
Somebody must have told me. I can't remember.
Whoever it was has become a shade imagined
From an ancient unrecoverable past.

Poem

The mind's whispering to itself is its necessity
To be itself and not to be any other,

If only for the moment as it passes.
It eats what it needs from the world around itself.

Slowly it makes its way floating through temperatures,
Degrees and other degrees of light and dark.

It moves through all things by virtue of its own
Characteristics. Mainly it is silent.

But when it utters a sound it is a sound
That others find hard to interpret, and that's known,

It supposes, only to another creature
It dreams of, so similar to itself as not

To have entirely separate identity.
Somewhere there may be such a creature.

Emerson said: "They may be real; perhaps they are."
Yet it also thinks it's the only one, and is lonely.

It can be silent and unknown except
To itself or not even known to itself

For long periods of time in sleepless revery.
It is never asleep during the long nights of sleep.

The Intention of Things

The death that lives in the intention of things
To have a meaning of some sort or other,

That means to come to something in the end,
It is the death that lives not finding the meaning

Of this or that object as it moves among them
Uncertainly, moving among the shadows,

The things that are like shadows, shadows of things,
The things the shadows of shadows, all in the effort

To put off the death that we are coming to.
The intention makes its way among its moments,

Choosing this object or that, uncertainly,
Somebody's body, or the leaves of a tree

On a summer night in a landscape somewhere else,
Under which something happened that made it different.

It is seeking to find the meaning of what they are.
But it moves uncertainly among them, the shadows,

The things that are like shadows, putting off
The death that is coming, that we are coming to.

It is the death that lives that makes the flower
Be what's it's going to be and makes it die,

And makes the musical phrase complete itself,
Or fail to complete itself, as Goethe said,

Writing a friend whose son had died in the Army:
"So you have had another terrible trial.

It's still, alas, the same old story: to live
Long is to outlive many; and after all,

We don't even know, then, what it was all about.
The answer to part of the riddle is, we each

Have something peculiarly our own, that we
Mean to develop by letting it take its course.

This strange thing cheats us from day to day, and so
We grow old without knowing how it happened or why."

It is the death that lives in the intention of things
To have a meaning of some sort or other;

Implacable, bewildered, it moves among us
Seeking its own completion, still seeking to do so,

But also putting it off, oh putting it off,
The death that is coming, that we are coming to.

The Birds

They're like the birds that gather in Virgil's lines
In the park at evening, sitting among the branches,
Not knowing who it is they're sitting among,

And trying out their little songs of who
They think they are and who their mother was;
And the evening sky that seemed to be a sheltering

Presence above them guaranteed by a poem,
Shifts above their heads and mutters darkly
About the weather and what is going to happen.

I don't know who it is I am sitting next to.
I can hear some notes tried out about the song
That they are trying to sing, but I don't know

What song it is, it's not exactly mine.

Prayer to the Gods of the Night

– Babylonian

The gates of the town are closed. The princes
Have gone to sleep. The chatter of voices

Has quieted down. Doorbolts are fastened.
Not until morning will they be opened.

The gods of the place, and the goddess,
Ishtar, Sin, Adad, and Shamash,

Have gone into the quiet of the sky,
Making no judgments. Only

The voice of a lone wayfarer
Calls out the name of Shamash or Ishtar.

Now house and field are entirely silent.
The night is veiled. A sleepless client

In the still night waits for the morning.
Great Shamash has gone into the sleeping

Heaven; the father of the poor,
The judge, has gone into his chamber.

May the gods of the night come forth – the Hunter,
The Bow, the Wagon, the Yoke, the Viper,

Irra the valiant, the Goat, the Bison,
Girra the shining, the Seven, the Dragon –

May the stars come forth in the high heaven.
Establish the truth in the ritual omen;

In the offered lamb establish the truth.

A Note about David Ferry

David Ferry was born in Orange, New Jersey, in 1924, and grew up and attended school in Maplewood, New Jersey. His undergraduate education at Amherst College was interrupted by a four-year stint in the US Army Air Force during World War II. He received his BA from Amherst in 1946, and went on to receive his PhD from Harvard University in 1955. It was during his years as a graduate student that he published his first poems, in the *Kenyon Review*.

From 1952 until his retirement in 1989 Ferry taught at Wellesley College. He now holds the title Sophie Chantal Hart Professor Emeritus of English at Wellesley. He has also taught creative writing at Boston University, and is a "Distinguished Visiting Scholar" at Suffolk University, Boston.

In 1958 Ferry married Anne Davidson, who became the eminent literary scholar and critic Anne Ferry. They had two children, Elizabeth Emma Ferry, an anthropologist, and Stephen Ferry, a photo-journalist. Before moving to his current home in Brookline, Massachusetts, Ferry lived across the Charles River in Cambridge, in a house whose first tenant, in 1842, had been the journalist and women's rights campaigner Margaret Fuller.

Ferry is the author of a book of criticism, *The Limits of Mortality: An Essay on Wordsworth's Major Poems* (1959), and five books of verse – *On the Way to the Island* (1960), *Strangers: A Book of Poems* (1983), *Dwelling Places: Poems and Translations* (1993), *Of No Country I Know: New and Selected Poems and Translations* (1999), and *Bewilderment: New and Selected Poems and Translations* (2012). He has also published five books of translation: *Gilgamesh: A New Rendering in English Verse* (1992), *The Odes of Horace: A Translation* (1997), *The Eclogues of Virgil* (1999), *The Epistles of Horace* (2001), and *The Georgics of Virgil* (2005).

Ferry has received many honors and awards, including John Simon Guggenheim and Ingram Merrill Fellowships, the Howard Morton Landon Translation Prize (for *The Epistles of Horace*) from the Academy of American Poets, the William Arrowsmith Translation Prize (for his rendering of Virgil's "First Eclogue") from *AGNI* magazine, the Golden Rose lifetime achievement award from the New England Poetry Club, the Teasdale Prize for Poetry, the Rebekah Johnson Bobbitt National Prize for Poetry (for *Of No Country I Know*) from the Library of Congress, the Lenore Marshall Poetry Prize (for *Of No Country I Know*) and the Ruth B. Lilly Prize for lifetime achievement from the Poetry Foundation. Ferry was awarded an honorary D.Litt. by Amherst College, and is a fellow of the American Academy of Arts and Sciences, and the Academy of American Poets.

He is presently at work on translations of Virgil's *Aeneid* and the *Satires* of Horace.

Other books from Waywiser

Other Books from Waywiser